# WATERCOLOR & Hand lettering

# Watercolor & Hand lettering

STEP-BY-STEP TECHNIQUES FOR MODERN ILLUSTRATED CALLIGRAPHY

Tanja Pöltl

DAVID & CHARLES

www.davidandcharles.com

# CONTENTS



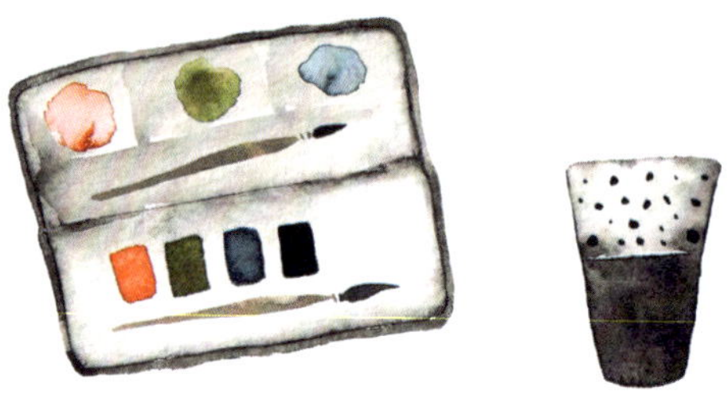

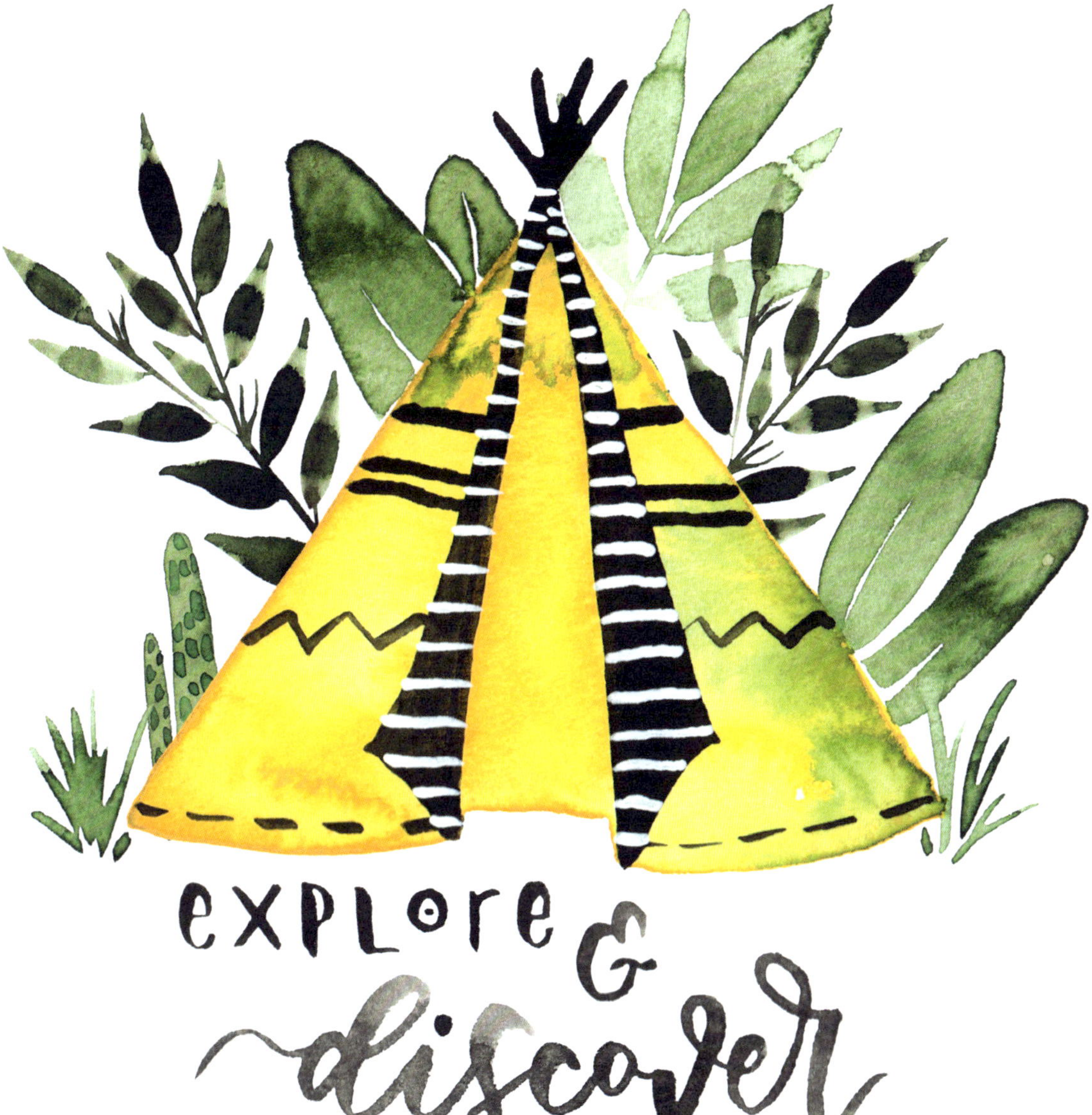
explore &
discover

# Foreword

## Hello, I'm Tanja.

My personal creative journey began not so long ago. In 2017, I started my 365-day project, "One Sketch a Day", just before the birth of our daughter. On maternity leave from my agency job, which had previously occupied over 40 hours of my week, my "work persona" was searching for something new that I could keep to in my everyday life as a #newmom.

You're now holding a book that contains my combined knowledge of hand lettering and watercolor. It's been shaped by my own initial attempts – the little steps, the larger milestones, the unintended blips – and my continued unfailing joy in experimentation. For me, the writing and designing of this book became more of an examination and questioning of my previous creative journey. One thing, however, is certain: I've progressed. But the question is: How did I do it?

My aim with this book is to promote your personal creative journey, whether you're at the very beginning or already in the middle. In addition, you can expect a lot of thoughts, information, and tips on topics, as well as attempts to answer often-asked questions such as: What is "reflection" and how can it help to improve your work? How can you make getting started easier? Is it okay to copy, and how can you learn from it?

I'll be providing you with lots of information about hand lettering and watercolor, including tips on materials, basic techniques, and useful tricks for fast and beautiful results.

The second part of this book contains 20 project ideas grouped under five themed categories. At this point, whether you're a beginner or more advanced, I'd like to invite you to venture out of your creative comfort zone from time to time. I've therefore designed the themed categories in a very different way, in order to immerse you in as diverse a world of designs as possible.

My motivation is to convince you to never stop seeing the world with fresh eyes, and I hope to encourage you to interpret it for yourself on paper. So get ready for the next step in your creative journey with the help of my knowledge, tips and ideas.

What are you waiting for?!

Tanja

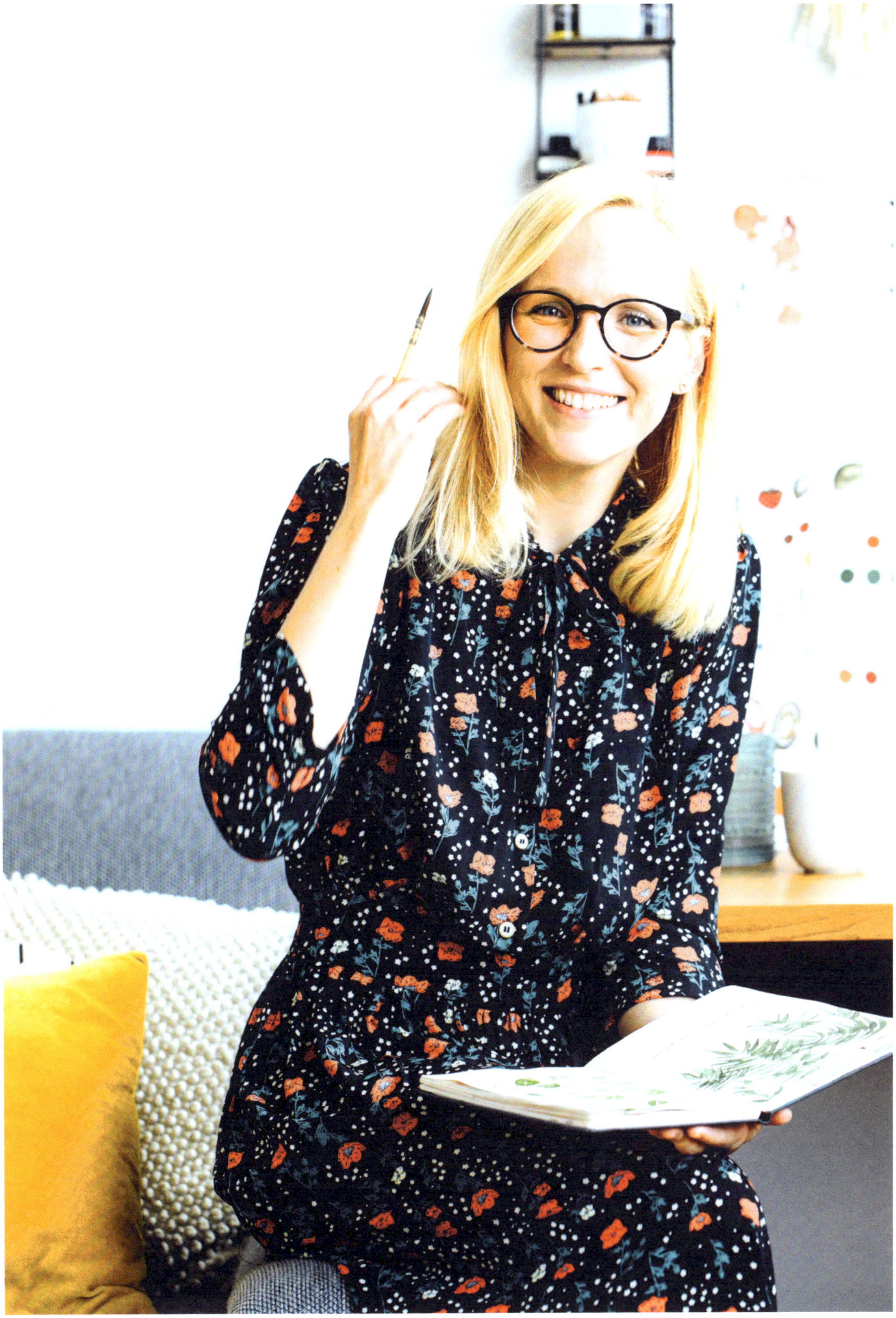

# Introduction

In this book, I'd like to accompany you on a very personal creative journey. By sharing my own experiences, I hope to inspire you and propel you forward.

## MY JOURNEY: 365 DAYS OF CREATIVE DOWNTIME

I'd like to start by briefly outlining my personal story, as I have found that often you can learn from other people's creative journeys, or even find yourself through them. I want to use my own experiences to show you that even the most enthusiastic starters need a little help along the way. Let me start where it all began for me – the beginning of my maternity leave, when I decided to take 20–30 minutes a day of creative downtime.

At that time, I had no specific ideas, but my motivation came from my enthusiasm for the topic of sketchnotes – something that has long fascinated me as a form of graphic recording. With the help of books, I was able to quickly learn how to draw doodles and use them for sketchnotes. I liked the idea of using doodles to visualize all the things in the world in the simplest way. So, there it was, my 365-day project: "One Sketch a Day".

Without really realizing it, I had begun my creative journey. After just a few sketchnoting attempts, I came across fashionable hand lettering, which really grabbed me. Self-taught, I immediately plunged into the wonderful world of hand and brush lettering materials...and failed miserably!

Countless wrong purchases resulted from my too easy-going approach. I didn't really understand what the problem was and why I was stuck. Why didn't my letterings look like those of the great artists on Instagram? After all, I had the same tools and understood the basics. Yet there was no sign of progress. Then, within six months, I discovered the combination of hand lettering with watercolor, which already appeared to be widespread.

And so, I too ventured into my first watercolor creations.

Along the way, I decided to let some professionals look over my work. I've attended three hand lettering and watercolor workshops to date, plus all the free and chargeable online courses and tutorials. No matter what the format, I was inspired in a different way every time, and each one helped me take a little step forward in developing my creative work. I found that a fresh look from the outside was good and afterwards I got the feeling that I knew more and more every day about what I was doing.

Almost a year had passed since my 365-day project began, and so, in June 2018, I founded **Die Handletterei**, and since then have been self-employed whilst continuing to work part-time in a media agency. This was a project dear to my heart, which I mainly started in order to pass on my accumulated knowledge via workshops, and to help beginners, in particular, avoid the stumbling blocks I had experienced and imposed on myself.

And now? I still continue to take my daily creative downtime, and for me, this continues to be the most important thing in my creative journey (of which I'm now more consciously aware). I don't follow a set plan with my creative work. Nevertheless, there are always exciting projects and commissions that challenge me afresh and shape me creatively. I really enjoy the carefree nature of my self-employed work, as well as the freedom of choice it gives me.

Now over to you... How about your creative journey? Are you still at the very beginning, or are you already in the middle of it?

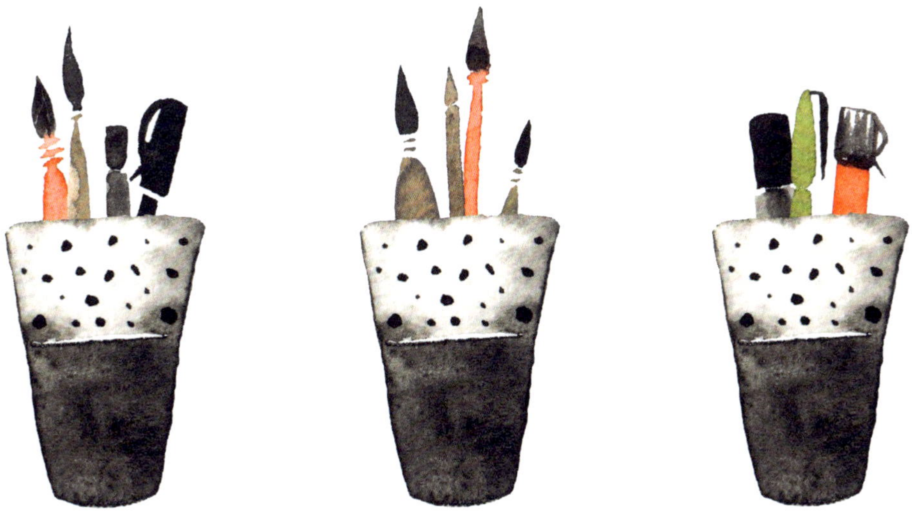

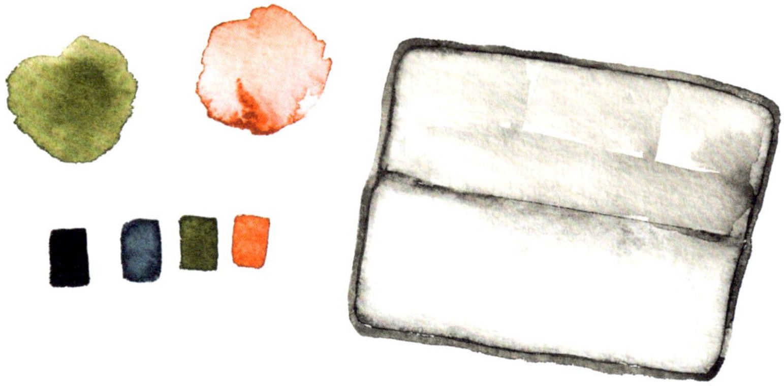

## YOUR CREATIVE JOURNEY

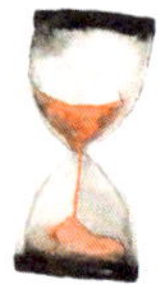

Some things come naturally, but many things don't. The following pages are intended to help you to ask essential questions, to take stock and enhance your creative process. I'd also like to give you tips on how to promote and challenge your creative development.

### START WHERE YOU ARE

Perhaps this strikes a chord: you see incredibly inspiring hand lettering compositions, illustrations and color combinations that grab you, styles that fit right into your own creative world - and then you have a go. You imitate, maybe even copy them, but somehow they don't look right; they look different from what you had hoped.

At this point, you feel as though you've taken two steps back. Yet what you have to be aware of is that those whom we consider to be great artists did not create great works overnight. Even those who have mastered their tools, who may have received training, and have in-depth (theoretical and practical) knowledge, were at exactly this point at ONE moment in THEIR creative journey. So, don't let this unsettle you or stop you from continuing. Give yourself time.

Your creative thoughts are sometimes a little ahead of what your practical knowledge permits, so to close the gap between "it looks like this" and "but I want it to look like that", the best thing you can do is to reflect.

### REFLECTION

Reflection in this case means close inspection. We often rewrite words or sayings numerous times or create illustrative designs on paper over and over again - and yet we're still not satisfied. Reflection should help you to determine what the specific reasons are if you're not satisfied with something, and where this is the case, in what way it could be changed or improved. Yet even close inspection has to be learned.

Here is a little checklist to help you reflect on your work. Ask yourself questions about the following areas:

## COLOR SCHEME

☐ Does the color combination look harmonious to you?

If not, what could you change?

- ☐ Reduce or increase the color?
- ☐ Change, darken or lighten the shades?
- ☐ Or maybe try a new color combination?

## HAND LETTERING

☐ Does the lettering take up enough space in your work? Should it be more in the background maybe, if the illustration is the actual focus of your piece?

☐ Does the lettering have a consistent and uniform effect? Look at, for example, the distances between the letters, review whether white spaces inside the letters are missing or are too large, and also observe the regularity of the downstrokes and upstrokes.

☐ Is the pen used right for the piece of work? Is there a pen choice that would be better/more effective for the paper used?

## ILLUSTRATION

☐ Does the illustration fit the lettering in terms of theme, style and size, etc.?

☐ Have you paid attention to the white spaces inside and around your illustration?

☐ Are you satisfied with the transparency or opacity of the paint(s)?

☐ Does the illustration appear consistent overall, or are there areas that appear too busy and shift the focus when you're looking at it? If so, what can you do to change that?

## DETAILS

☐ Have you put the finishing touches to your work with details? Or maybe there are too many and your work appears overloaded?

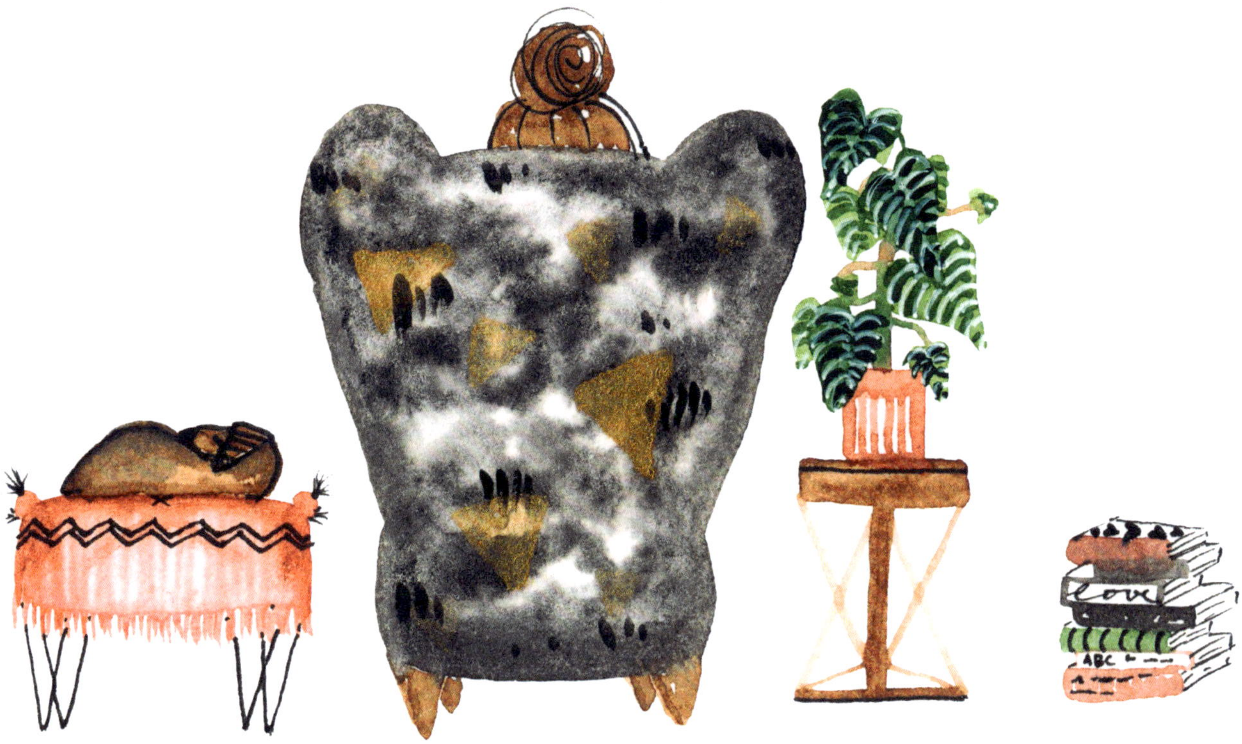


TIP: *"It's all about the details" – I can still hear these words from one of the online courses I undertook on Skillshare, an American platform that offers, in my opinion, good and above all user-friendly, chargeable, online video tutorials. These take the form of classes on a wide range of creative and business topics (you can also watch the classes via an app on your phone or tablet). Details can help you to visually close white spaces that are too large within your work, give individual elements more character and also emphasize the focus of your piece. I'll show you how to do this, and how to liven up your work through detail, using the projects in the second half of this book.*

When reflecting on your work, try to put into words, as specifically as you can, what changes might help make your work more harmonious, or that might make it more like your ideas. You can then consciously, and also unconsciously, include these points in your next pieces.

## STARTING MADE EASY/EASIER

What do you do if you're sitting in front of a blank sheet of paper and just don't know how or where to start?

Ask yourself about the purpose of your creative session at the outset, as it makes a difference in our minds whether we want to create a final piece, i.e. a final work to be hung up, given away or maybe even sold, or whether it's purely about the creative process we want to engage in for a few minutes. In my view, the less you think about the end result, the easier it is to get started.

Before you actually sit down for your creative session, think of at least one design theme in advance. For this step, the subject areas can be very general, such as plants, landscapes, interiors, wildlife, etc., or even more specific themed ideas, such as tropical plants, a botanical garden, an urban jungle, or an underwater world, etc.

With a design in your head, it's much easier to take the first step in your creative session – for example, by starting to put together and mix suitable colors. If you're still hesitating to take the first brush or pen stroke, start on another sheet of paper with a few warm-up exercises. Try out your chosen colors, practice brush strokes, create the first letters. Warm-up exercises make it easier to begin because you've more or less already started mentally.

TIP: *Try to step outside your creative comfort zone from time to time by allowing more spontaneity in your work and by simply starting a piece without pencil strokes. You'll be surprised by the result.*

## COPYING AND LEARNING

In my view, for practice purposes, copying – and learning from it – is a perfectly legitimate, even an important step in a creative journey.

Some time ago, I took away a thought from one of the episodes of 3 Point Perspective (a podcast that covers the topic of illustration), which, when discussing the controversial subject of "copying others", said that when you learn a musical instrument, you start by practicing the works of others and not by composing your own work.

Thus, you shouldn't hesitate to take inspiration from the works of others and to copy some of them too, especially when it comes to learning a technique. **N.B.** In terms of copyright, you're not allowed to publish works that you've copied/imitated exactly, or to use them commercially either.

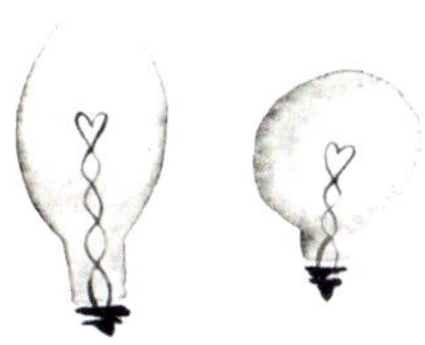

*TIP: Think about the works of others when on your creative journey, and not just your own. Ask yourself why you like another artist's work. What makes the work great for you? Is it the detail? Is it the color scheme? The technique? The hand lettering style? Or is it that the motifs are presented in a simplified way? Sometimes, it's just a few things that make something particularly beautiful and appealing. The WHY is exactly what you want to take away to consider how you can use it in your own work.*

## DOCUMENT YOUR PROGRESS

There'll come a point when you might not be sure when you last made any progress, or whether you're developing at all, and you may even question whether this is the right direction to pursue. With all these thoughts, a means of documentation will help you make your creative development visible.

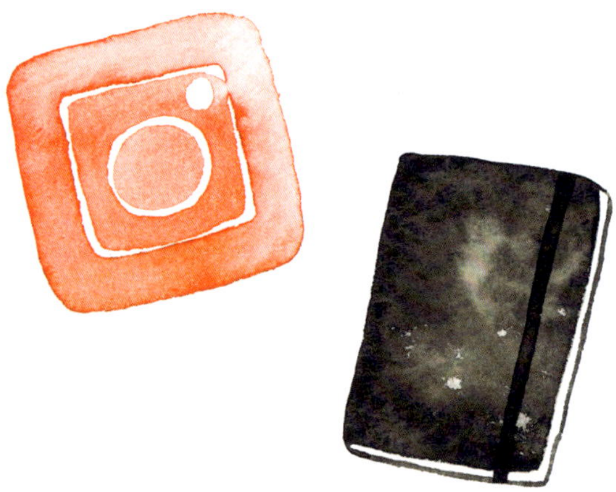

This can be a creative folder or a file, a journal, or even, how I do it, by using Instagram. It can be an incredible motivation to see where you were maybe a year, or even just a few months, ago and where you are today. You can also use this recall process as an opportunity to reflect – in this case, not just on individual pieces, but on your creative journey to date. Try to put your progress into words in order to decide on the next step and where you want to put your focus in future.

## FINDING, GATHERING AND USING INSPIRATION

Inspiration is difficult to pin down. How do we know what actually inspired us and when? Is it the works of other artists in our field or even completely different (creative) areas? Is it our own emotional world that opens our eyes to other things again, or is it our current phase of life? Are we influenced by our mood or how we feel that particular day? Is it experiences, our leisure activities, the people around us, or simply everyday situations? I could continue this list indefinitely.

There are many ways to gather inspiration and make it visible and attainable, just when you need it. These can be your own pinboards on Pinterest, or saved images, sorted into folders, in the Instagram app; or it can be your own ongoing photography of images sorted into photo folders on your phone or computer. Whether it's countryside views, photographed excerpts from magazines, or simply recording the flair and style of places where you just feel comfortable, try to use as many sources as possible, and don't limit yourself to a single channel of inspiration.

**TIP:** *You may prefer to create an inspiration collection by hand, rather than digitally, e.g. in the form of an herbarium, a collage, a magazine collection, or a journal.*

You can then decide how this orderly arrangement of inspiration is reflected in your pieces. It can be colors, shapes from nature, a whole image (photo), scenery, or even a style of writing. The important thing is that you use all the types of inspiration as a source of ideas and support for your creative session and not something that you copy exactly.

## ESTABLISHING YOUR OWN STYLE

What is meant by "your own style"? Objectively speaking, you could say it has to do with a certain degree of consistency, memorability, differentiation from others and, most importantly, a personal touch that is always reflected in a certain way.

It may not be easy to put your finger on what your style is, but one thing I firmly believe is that you'll probably never have one single style. Even if you've discovered for yourself recurring, memorable and differentiating elements, including colors or topics, it's very likely that things from your life and your living environment will resonate and become visible in your personal style. This doesn't mean that you'll constantly change your creative look, but that your own style is pretty much the same as your creative journey: it's a never-ending process.

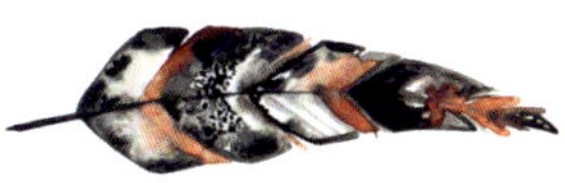

How and when do you create your own style? It's not something that just happens overnight. Nevertheless, you can help the process by setting a basic foundation for yourself and constantly questioning it; keep working on it, change some things, allow others to remain. What am I talking about here? Establish your own color scheme, for example, or focus on one or more writing styles. A design theme that is followed consistently helps to develop memorability.

**TIP:** *Establishing your own style is also very much a question of what you decide not to do. Not every design, color combination or saying will fit your particular style.*

What personally helped me to follow a style – and I'm still working on it by the way – was trying to put my own desired style into words. Try it yourself: what associations, characteristics and words describe and resonate with your style when you consider one of your works?

However, when you're starting out on your creative path, it's important to experiment – don't try to achieve any one particular style. The fastest way to find out what suits you, what reflects your personality and what comes closest to expressing your creative thoughts is achieved through experimentation and practice. Try a wide variety of materials – often it's these that help you to find new creative possibilities and ideas, and they too contribute to the development of your own style.

## YOUR CREATIVE SPACE FOR EVERYDAY USE

If your creative materials are always available, it's much easier to sit down for even 15 minutes and pick up a brush or pen. Sometimes, you don't have a spare area to keep things set out – in which case, think about collecting everything together and keeping it well organized in a creative box or other creative system (e.g. a small trolley). The fewer the actions required to clear up and tidy away, the more likely you are to get started.

TIP: *Tidy up your area or mobile creative system after each of your creative sessions. Experience has shown that disorganized chaos can also prevent you from starting a creative session in the first place.*

I hope that in this chapter, I've been able to give you some hints and thoughts for your creative journey. Over the coming pages, I'd like to give you an insight into the materials and the techniques of hand lettering and watercolor, so that you can get started with the projects in this book.

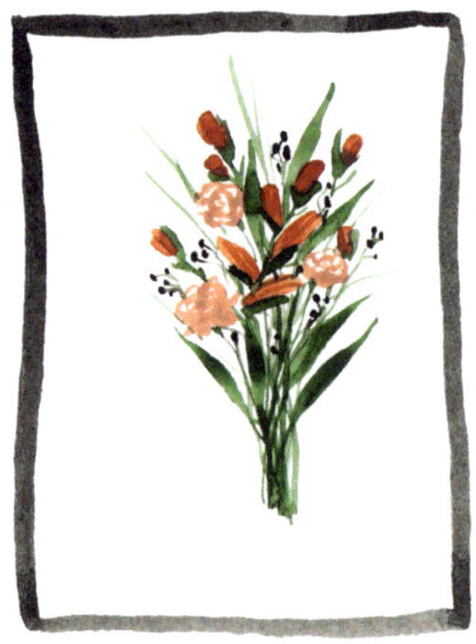

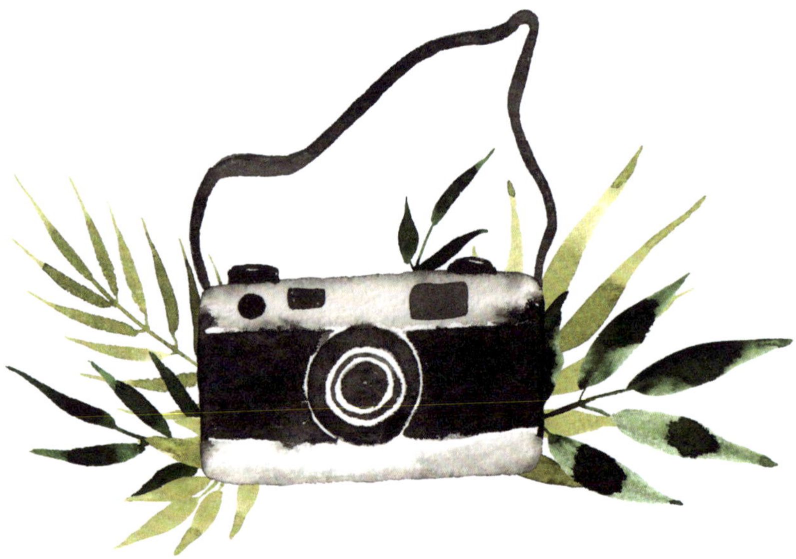

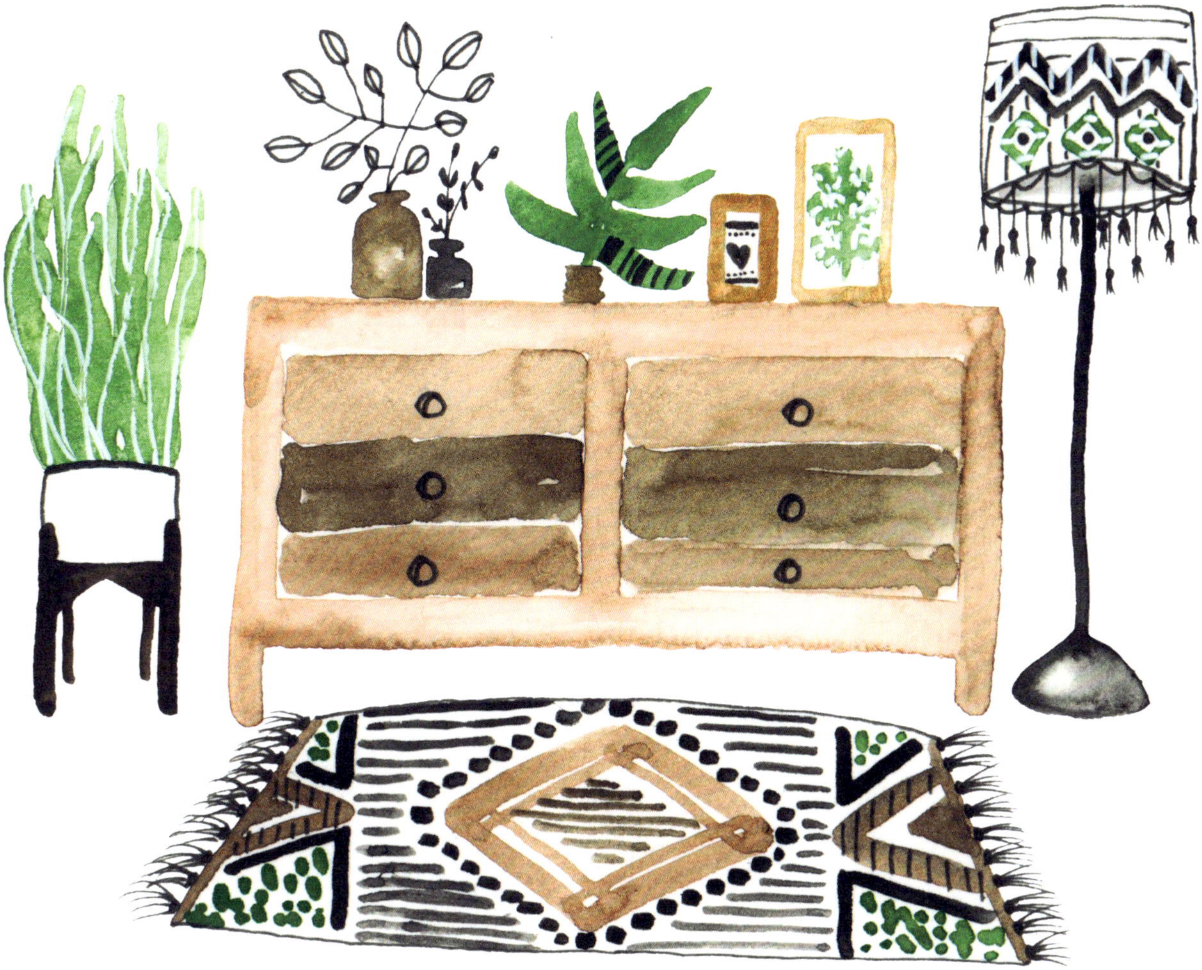

# BASICS

Before you get to work, I'd like to equip you with a few basics to help you prepare for implementing your ideas and projects. The focus of this section is, therefore, materials (pens, paints, paper), helpful hand lettering tips, and the most important watercolor techniques.

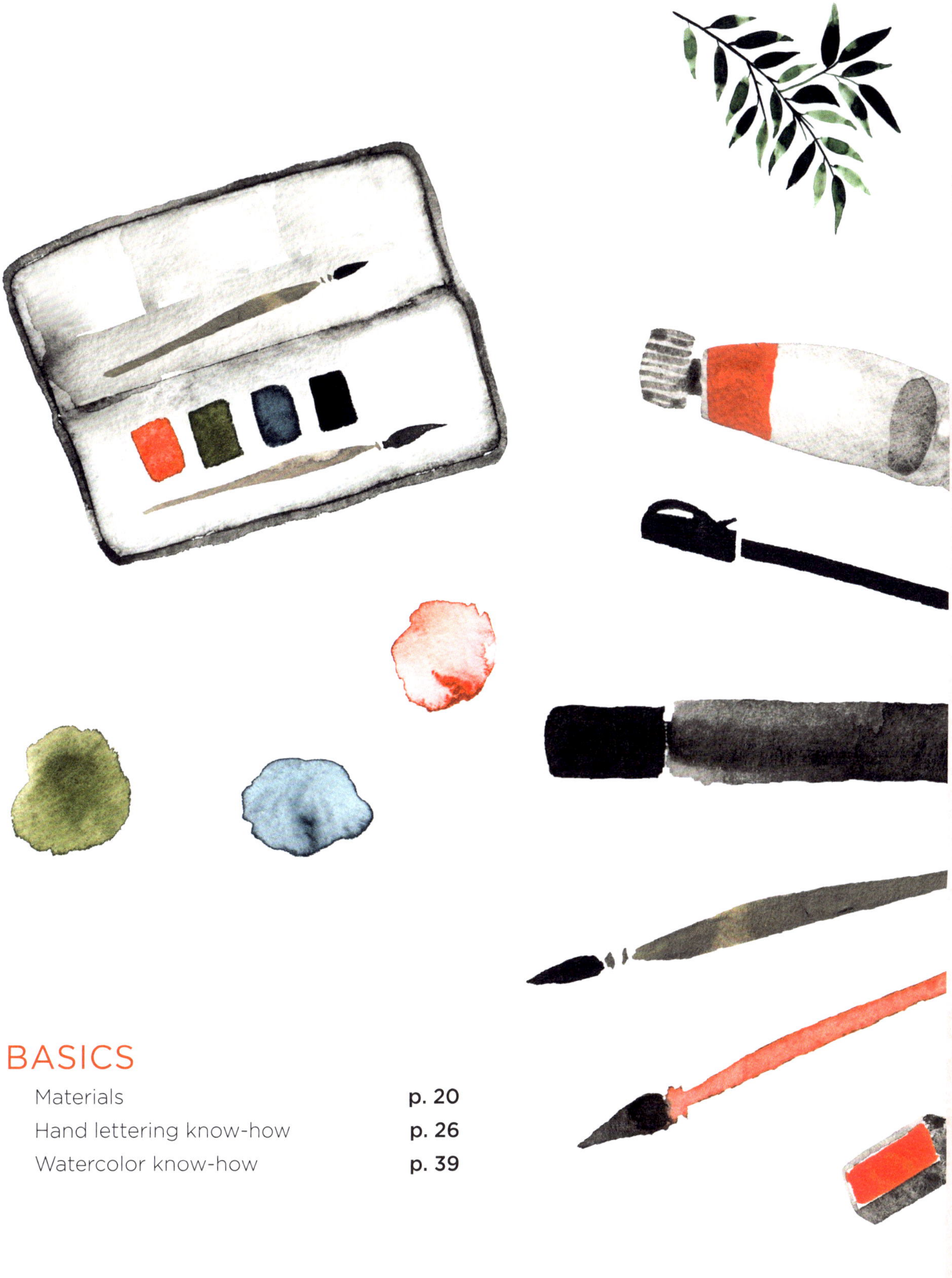

# BASICS

# Materials

There are so many materials to explore. In this chapter, I refer to brands that I personally prefer, but many others are available. When purchasing materials, pay attention to quality and product attributes. Decide for yourself which are best for you.

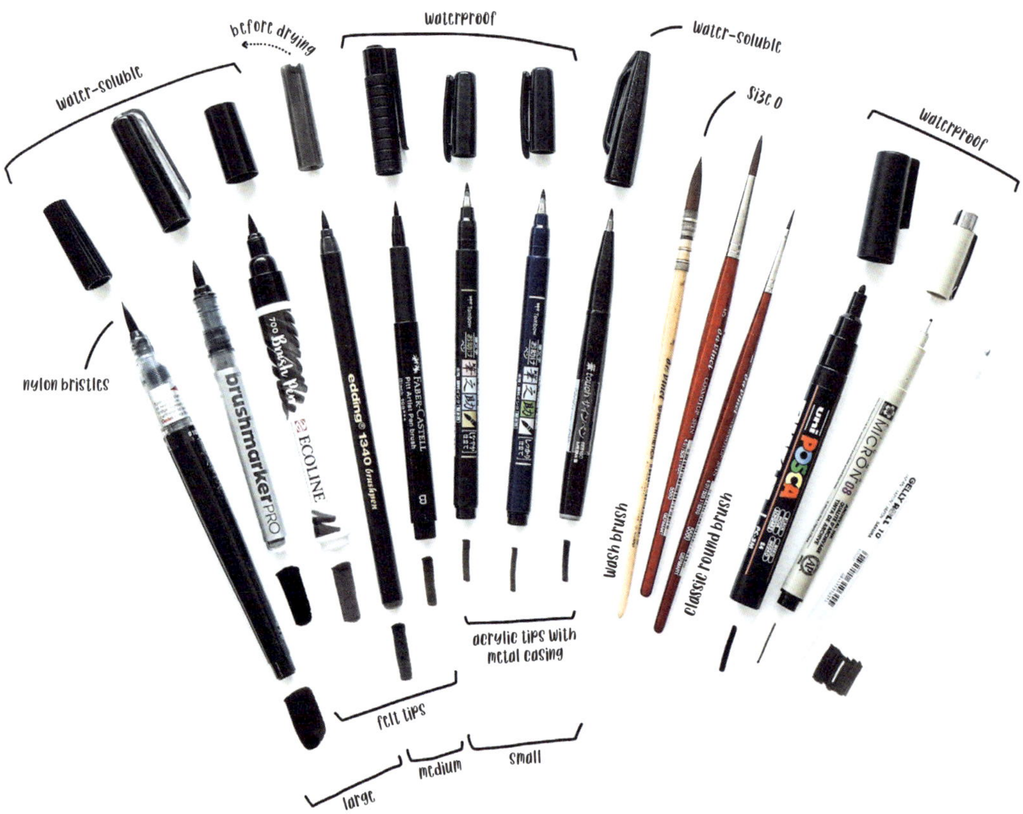


**From left to right:**
Pentel Arts Color Brush Pen
Karin Brushmarker Pro
Royal Talens Ecoline Brush Pen
Edding 1340 Brush Pen
Faber-Castell Pitt Artist Pen Brush Nib
Tombow Fudenosuke Soft (WS-BS)
Tombow Fudenosuke Hard (WS-BH)
Pentel Arts Brush Tip Sign Pen
Da Vinci 488, Size 0 (Spin-Synthetics)
Da Vinci 5880, Size 5 (Cosmotop-Spin)
Da Vinci 5880, Size 1 (Cosmotop-Spin)
Uni Posca Paint Marker
Sakura Pigma Micron Pen
Sakura Gelly Roll Gel Pen

# HAND LETTERING PENS

## BRUSH PENS

When it comes to choosing a brush pen, I've an all-time favorite: the **Tombow Fudenosuke Soft (WS-BS)**. This brush pen has a smaller and fairly robust brush tip and is especially suitable for beginners who are keen to learn hand lettering. The black ink is waterproof, which means that the pen is particularly good for watercolor illustrations.

If you want to buy some new brush pens, check out a few basic attributes – these can make your purchase decision a little easier:

### Size

Basically, you've a choice between **small**, **medium** and **large brush pen tips**. Bear in mind that the bigger the brush pen tip, the bigger your lettering will also need to be.

### Nature

The majority of brush pens have a **felt tip** that mimics the shape of a classic brush tip. When using a felt-tip brush pen you should not use paper that's too rough as felt tips can easily fray and subsequently leave unsightly streaks in your lettering.

There are also brush pens with tips made of individual bristles in **nylon**. Such brush pen tips are less beginner-friendly for lettering purposes, as they are very flexible and it's more difficult to control the stroke.

A few brush pens (including my favorite), have an **acrylic tip with metal casing**. This differs from the conventional felt tip in that it is more robust, which means that it doesn't fray and it can also be used on rougher paper. In addition to the Tombow Fudenosuke Soft, this also applies to the **Tombow Fudenosuke Hard (WS-BH)**, which has a slightly harder brush tip. The same is true of the **Pentel Arts Brush Tip Sign Pen** (also known as the **Pentel Touch**), which in terms of the hardness of the tip is comparable with the Tombow Fudenosuke Soft, although it is water-soluble rather than waterproof.

### Shape retention

The shape retention of a brush pen generally refers to the ability of the brush pen tip to maintain its shape despite varying exertion of pressure. You can easily test the shape retention by pressing the brush pen down to determine the **degree of softness** of the pen tip. For brush pens with high shape retention, i.e. with a lower degree of softness, the stroke is easier to make than with brush pens with lower shape retention, i.e. with a higher degree of softness.

### Ink

Inks in brush pens (and in other pens too) can be **waterproof** or **water-soluble**. Waterproof means that your lettering cannot be smudged or blended if the ink comes into contact with water after being applied to paper. Whereas water-soluble inks do exactly that: you can paint over the ink with a paintbrush or water-tank brush and achieve blending or watercolor effects in this way. **N.B.** The often-used term "water-based" says nothing about whether a pen is waterproof or water-soluble. Water-based pens are simply child-friendly and odorless.

## PIGMENT LINERS

My favorite pigment liner is the **Sakura Pigma Micron**. Why? In comparison with other pigment liners, this scores higher in my view due to its high-grade, rich black. The special thing about such pigment liners in general is that, in addition to their high pigment density, they're lightfast. This means that they have a high color fastness and they won't fade or yellow due to UV light. In terms of using this ink with watercolor paints, it should be noted that it is waterproof. Personally, I use the stroke widths 0.3 and 0.8 most often.

TIP: *Faber-Castell, Staedtler, Edding, Pentel and other brands also have non-fade, waterproof pigment liners in their range. Just look around and decide which brand you prefer.*

## PIGMENT MARKERS

The **Uni Posca Paint Marker** has several advantages that I don't want you to overlook. Its ink is opaque and lightfast, and I'm a fan of its matte look once it has dried. You can use this marker not only on paper, but actually on all surfaces. **N.B.** On rough surfaces, the marker is permanent (meaning that the ink can no longer be removed with water); however, on smooth surfaces, for example glass, the ink can easily be wiped off with water. This marker is available with different tips and in different colors. I prefer the usual round tip in black, but as always, I recommend that you try out different markers and decide for yourself which one suits you best.

## GEL PENS

I use a white gel pen mainly for adding highlights to illustrations, and also to correct little mistakes and inaccuracies in lettering. A consistent and opaque stroke is the be-all and end-all of such gel pens, and that's exactly what **Sakura's Gelly Roll Gel Pen** can do in my eyes. It is available in different stroke widths and colors.

# WATERCOLOR PAINT

When purchasing watercolor paint, pay particular attention to the density of the pigment. Highly pigmented watercolor paint, so-called artist's watercolor paint, is usually fairly expensive, but in my opinion it is worth the investment. Working with highly pigmented artist's paint - compared to less pigmented (water) color - doesn't just make a difference to the painting process itself. There is also a clearly recognizable difference in the result and in the durability of your work. Artist's watercolor paint is basically more colorful, depending on the shade and the pigments used; it also more opaque and, above all, it is lightfast. Whether you use watercolor paint in pans or tubes is a matter of preference, but it tends to make more sense to use tubes if you want to work over greater areas or with more opacity. You could also fill your empty pans with watercolor paint from tubes, let them dry and thus adjust your repertoire of watercolor paints. The effect is the same. I myself prefer the pans from **Schmincke Horadam Aquarell Watercolor Pan Set**, which I add to my paint box and rearrange whenever I wish. Watercolor paint in pans is usually available in two sizes: whole and half pans.

# BRUSHES

Watercolor brushes come in a wide variety of designs in terms of the shape of the brush tip. I'd like to introduce you here to the two types of brushes that I use most often.

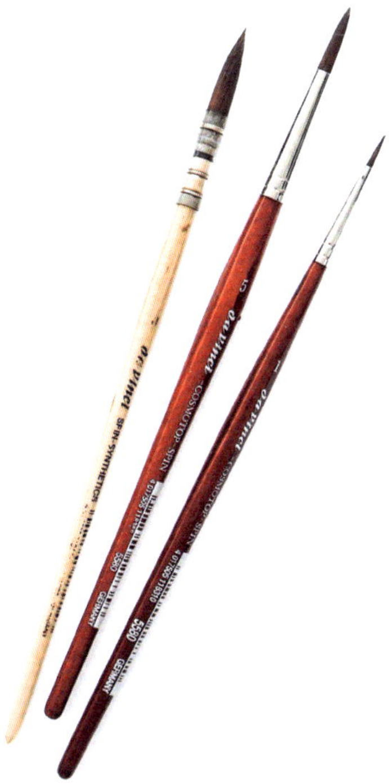

## ROUND BRUSH

The round brush features a brush tip that comes to a point, and both fine and wider brush strokes are possible. This flexibility of stroke width is very practical, for example, when painting leaves. In addition, it's possible to use the brush not only as a painting tool, but also for drawing an illustration (in the form of contours or lines, for example) by using the brush as if it were a more flexible pen.

## WASH BRUSH

The wash brush is in principle also a kind of round brush (characterized by a converging tip), but this type of brush has more bound bristles. As its name suggests, the wash brush is able to absorb far more water and can be used in particular to vastly water down paint that has been applied to paper. Personally, I use this brush in most cases like a classic round brush, for illustrating leaves, for example, and other objects too. The fact that the wash brush can absorb more water (and also more paint) is evident in the results, when compared to the use of a standard watercolor round brush.

TIP: *When buying brushes, pay attention to the degree of flexibility and softness in the bound bristles (whether they be synthetic or real hair), as for watercolor painting, your brush should be able to absorb and hold a lot of water. Also, pay attention to the quality. An investment in high-quality brushes pays off in the painting process.*

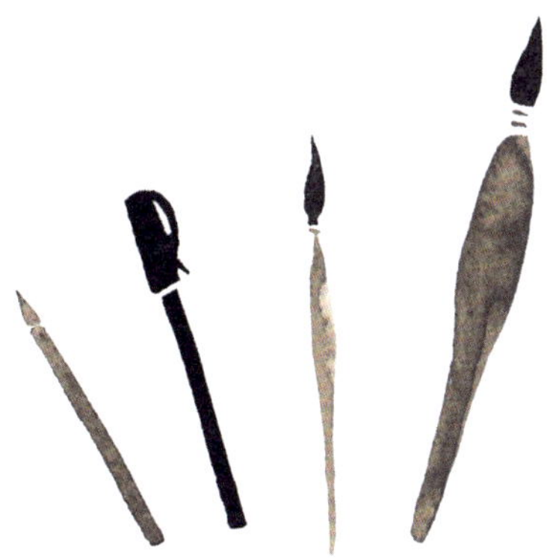

# PAPER

The choice of paper types is vast. In this section, I'd like to share with you a selection of those that I myself use. Ultimately, however, you can only decide which paper is the best for your purpose by trying the possibilities out for yourself.

## PAPER FOR HAND LETTERING

Not every hand lettering pen works well with every type of paper. Conventional copier paper, for example, can significantly shorten the life of your felt-tip brush pen, because the felt tip can easily fray if the surface is too rough. So, it's best to use very smooth laser printer paper. Alternatively, there is also specific hand lettering paper (for example, from Hahnemühle); this type of paper has a very smooth surface and saves the tips of your brush pens. However, neither this nor laser printer paper are suitable for wet techniques, such as watercolor.

TIP: *Tracing paper is very suitable for practicing letters and alphabets. For all the exercises and alphabets in the Hand Lettering Know-How chapter, you can place a sheet of tracing paper over the relevant section of this book and practice the particular stroke.*

## PAPER FOR WATERCOLOR

There are various types of watercolor paper that mainly differ in their surface structure, and the type you choose will influence the result of your watercolor art. The following terms will most likely be encountered when buying watercolor paper. In general, there are three different types of watercolor paper that describe the quality of the paper surface and also its associated water absorption capacity: **smooth**, **matte** and **rough**.

In many cases, smooth watercolor paper is accompanied by the terms **satin** or **hot-pressed**. Hot-pressed watercolor paper absorbs water less quickly than, for example, matte or rough paper. A smooth, satin-based surface can be particularly advantageous for detailed and delicate work.

Matte or (very) rough watercolor paper is in most cases associated with the term **cold-pressed**. These watercolor paper types absorb water in the painting process significantly faster; this means that they usually also require wetter work. The difference between matte and rough is shown by the paper grain or texture. Rough watercolor paper is coarser than matte and has a much thicker structure.

You may also be confronted with the term **torchon** when buying watercolor paper. This describes a very rough, almost linen-like watercolor paper. I would advise against this type of paper if you are a beginner; and, if you want to work more precisely with watercolor paint, or would like to do hand lettering on the paper, this is not the best choice.

## MIXED MEDIA PAPER

The combination of hand lettering and watercolor sometimes makes the paper and pen selection difficult. On the one hand, you want to achieve beautiful and well defined watercolor effects, while on the other hand, you need to spare the brush pen tips.

A good solution in such cases is mixed media paper. This type of paper, as the name suggests, allows the use of different techniques, including wet techniques such as watercolor. Although the result differs from that achieved with watercolor paper, mixed media paper makes lettering easier in most cases due to the rather smooth surface structure. My favorite is **Canson Imagine Mix Media Paper (120lb/200gsm)**.

TIP: *If you still want to hand letter on watercolor paper, as I do in most cases, it's best to use brush pens with more robust brush tips like the Tombow Fudenosuke Soft and Hard.*

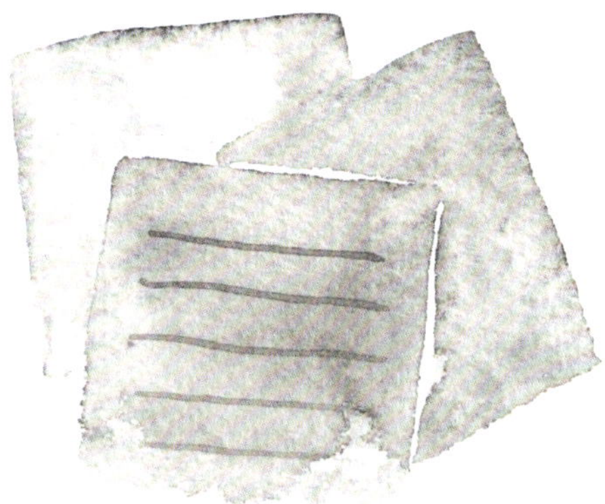

## GO PENCIL-FREE

With this book, I consciously want to spur you on to have no limits to your creativity; leave your pencil in the box and let your brush do its work. Set aside any attitude of perfection in terms of detail, perspective or realistic representation. A loose style is widely used in the field of watercolor illustration. This may mean that you need to give up a bit of control and that the results may not be completely predictable, yet you'll be surprised to see what you conjure up.

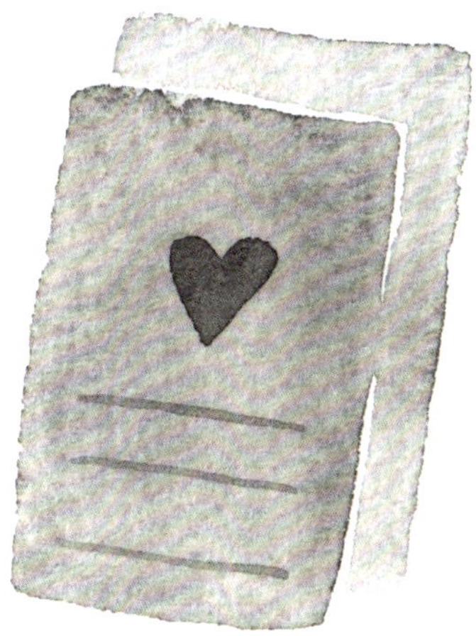

# Hand Lettering Know-How

In this chapter, you'll find a veritable treasure trove of thoughts on the essentials of hand lettering. In addition, I'll give you valuable tips on how to quickly get beautiful lettering results, as well as advice on making your script more harmonious overall.

## HAND LETTERING BASICS

### POSTURE AND HOLDING THE PEN

Even your posture plays an essential role in hand lettering. If you're too cramped or bent over, this can have an immediate effect on your script. Try to adopt good posture, place both feet on the floor, relax, and don't forget to breathe. Sometimes, you'll notice that you're holding your breath in concentration and this may translate in your lettering to a shaky or unclean stroke.

Correct pen posture is another essential point, which you should heed from the outset. The handling of brush pens, in particular, can be very challenging due to the flexible brush tip. Brush pens require more support to ensure you have consistent control over the flexible pen tip.

**Here's how to hold your brush pen correctly:** As a starting position, take your brush pen in your hand like an ordinary pen. In most cases, the pen now lies in the hollow between the thumb and the index finger. That's exactly where the brush pen shouldn't be lying. Therefore, take the rear end of the brush pen and simply place the pen a bit further along the index finger, while still holding the pen forward normally as before.

Now your brush pen is stable on your index finger, and you can control the necessary pressure for downstrokes and upstrokes, so that even the transitions between these two strokes appear clean and elegant. So, now you know how to hold your brush pen, let's continue by introducing the two key brush lettering strokes.

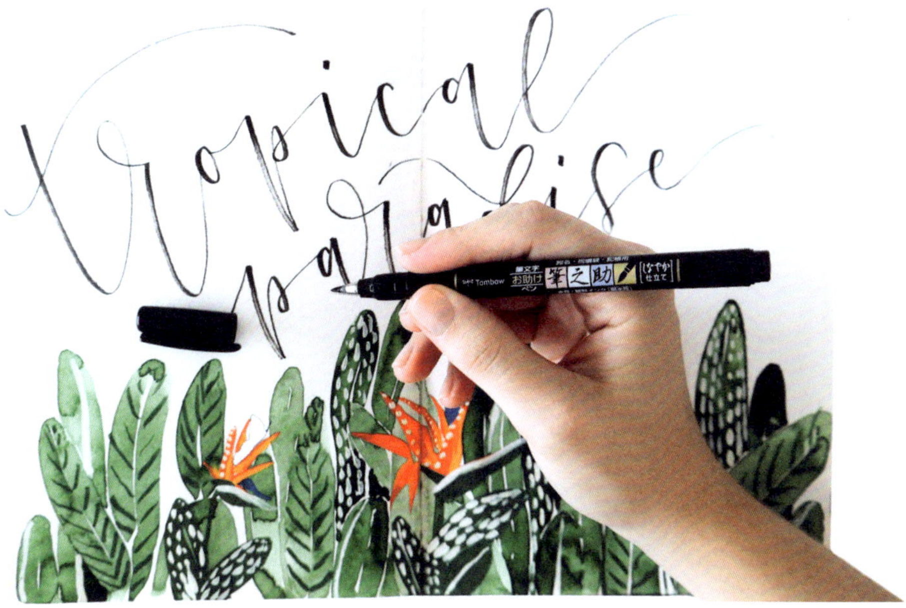


## DOWNSTROKES AND UPSTROKES

Knowledge of downstrokes and upstrokes is the be-all and end-all in hand lettering. Essential for brush lettering, a special kind of hand lettering, you can also apply this knowledge to other styles of writing too.

**Here's how to make these key strokes:**
With strokes from top to bottom (downstrokes), you put more pressure on your brush pen and a thicker stroke is the result. For strokes from bottom to top (upstrokes), you reduce the pressure of your brush pen tip on the paper to create thinner lines.

TIP: *To make the most of the flexible tip of your brush pen and to place it correctly on the paper (especially for the downstroke), let the pen tip point in the direction of 9 to 10 o'clock. Make sure you don't place the pen at too steep an angle to the paper. Firstly, it doesn't do the (felt) brush tip any good, and secondly, you lose control over the movement of the brush tip when placing it vertically. This also applies to placing the pen too flat. No matter which brush pen you're using, always try it out on paper first, to determine the incline or angle to the paper that is best for spreading out the tip of the pen and that is most comfortable.*

# WARM-UP EXERCISES

Tracing paper is particularly useful for practicing the strokes, letters and alphabets in this section. You can place this on the book and follow the stroke guide given. If you like, you can also do the exercises on a blank sheet of paper instead. This option is especially useful if you want to letter with a larger brush pen tip than the one I use, which is the Tombow Fudenosuke Soft (WS-BS).

## EXERCISE 1: DOWNSTROKES AND UPSTROKES

Start with a few downstrokes and upstrokes to get a feel for your brush pen and practice correct pen holding.

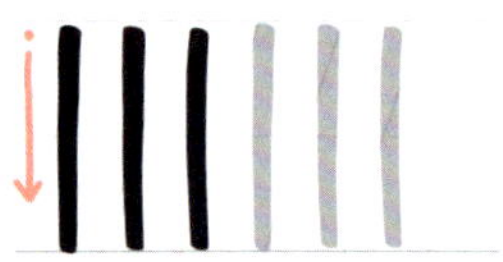

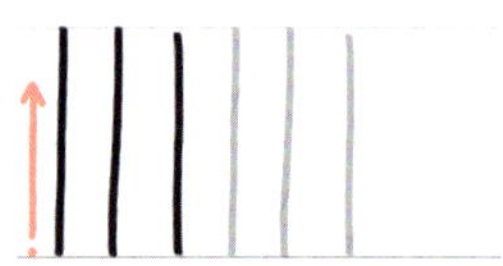

Perhaps you're not quite sure yet whether the respective stroke widths for downstrokes and upstrokes are wide or thin enough? There is no right and wrong way here. You determine the contrast between the stroke widths.

TIP: *If you opted for a wider stroke for the downstroke and a thinner stroke for the upstroke and have thus defined a contrast, stick to it with your particular lettering and pay attention to the uniformity of this contrast.*

## EXERCISE 2: OVER- AND UNDERTURNS

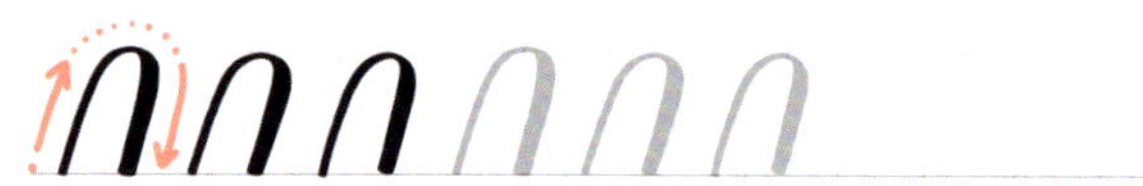

Start by drawing the overturns from bottom left, with an upstroke over the overturn and down to bottom right with a downstroke.

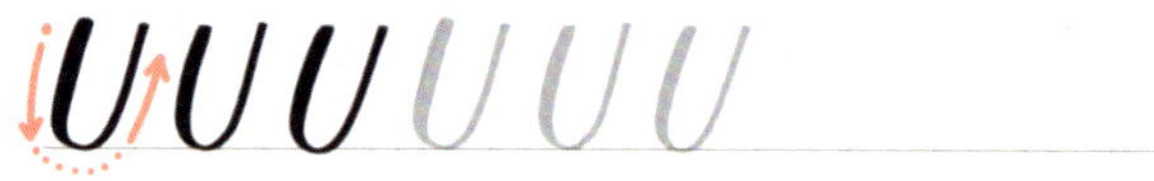

Try to draw the underturn in a U-shape, starting with a downstroke from the top left, continuing with the underturn and pulling the upstroke thinly upwards. Make sure that the rounded area (indicated here by a dotted line) has a thin stroke, and is not the width of the downstroke.

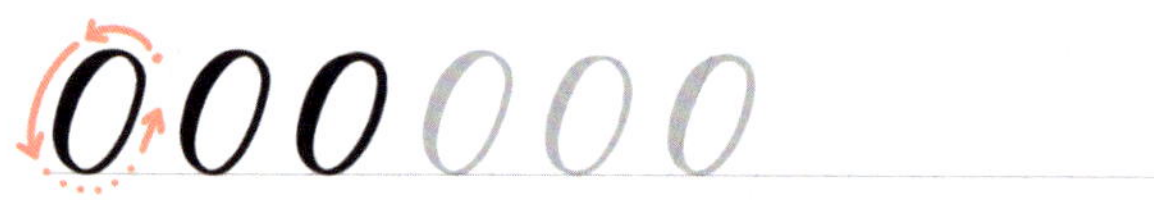

Place the brush pen at the marked point, slightly offset to the right at the top, so that you can do the thin rounded area well and the circle can be closed seamlessly.

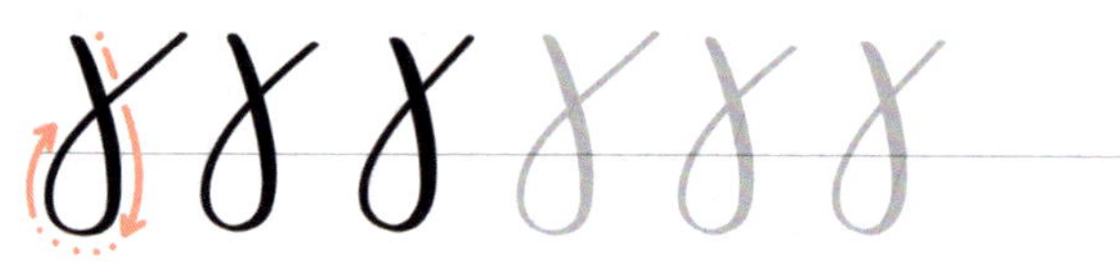

Once again, starting at the marked point, run the loop so that first a thick and then a thinner line is created.

# PRACTICING LETTERS

For the purpose of practicing, I've categorized the letters for you in groups that are similar in their execution. This allows you to optimize the uniformity of the letters and your script right from the start.

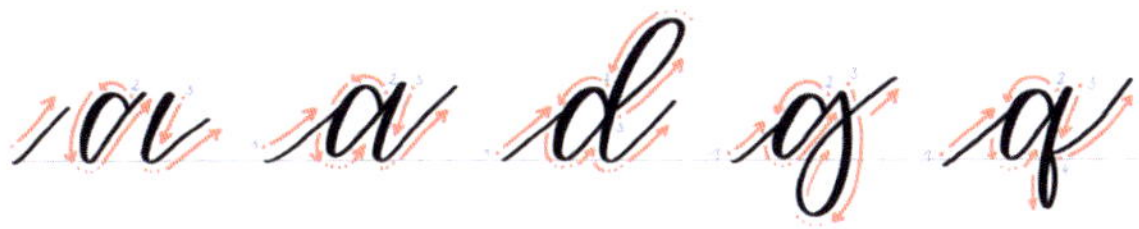

## HERE'S HOW TO DO IT

Start each letter with a little upstroke as a connector stroke, that is, as an imagined connection from the previous letter to the letter you want to letter next. This will help you to merge the letters into words later.

For this letter group ("a", "d", "g" and "q"), don't draw the so-called belly completely round (as you did in the warm-up exercise for "o" in Exercise 2: Over- and Underturns), but try to finish it with a slightly oblique oval. Also, drag the upstroke a little past the point at which you started. This enables you to add more white space to your hand lettering.

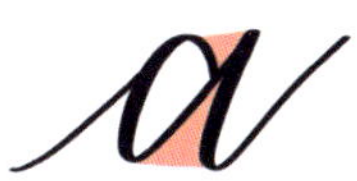

By generously creating white spaces within the letters, as well as between individual letters and words, your lettering will look more professional and visibly different from your hand-writing script. Sufficient white space also serves to promote overall readability.

TIP: *If you draw the downstroke for the descender of the letter "g" (i.e. the loop below) slightly to the right instead of dragging the downstroke strictly vertically downwards, you'll create additional white space between the loop and the belly of the letter.*

Here, as with the overturns and underturns in the Warm-Up Exercises: Exercise 2, pay attention to creating a thin stroke with certain areas of the letter. For example, with the "g", it should be clearly visible in the belly of the letter, as well as in the lower part of the descender. This also applies to the upper part of the ascender of the "d". You can achieve a thin stroke by reducing the pressure on the brush pen tip in good time, thus creating a clean transition between the downstroke and the upstroke.

Always put the brush pen down at every marked point, take your time, think about the next stroke ahead and only then continue to letter. In this way, you can concentrate on the clean execution of downstrokes and upstrokes, and better control distances and white spaces.

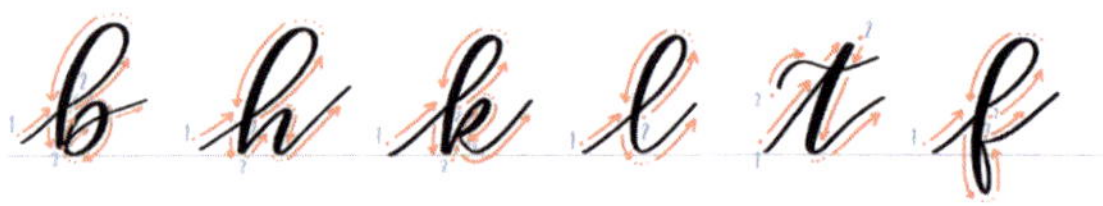

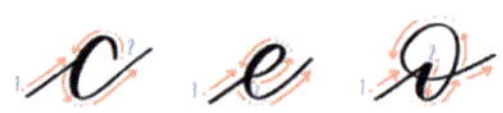

You should avoid forming letters (or words) in one go.

## HERE'S HOW TO DO IT

For all the letters in this letter group, except for the "t", take a break after the first little upstroke, before you draw the loop, i.e. the ascender, and deliberately reset the pen at this point. As you can see, there is a slight kink at the point where you start again. This makes it easier for you to drag the loop upwards than if you were to drag the stroke from the beginning to the end.

For all these letters, try to slightly curve the longer downstroke, rather than drawing it strictly straight. This will give the letters even more dynamism.

For more white space with the letters "b", "h" and "k", put the brush pen back on the lower right point after the first downstroke and draw the subsequent upstroke away to the right.

TIP: *You can draw the letters without loops too. Whichever option you decide on, try to maintain it as consistently as possible within the lettering as this is how you'll achieve more harmony and consistency in your script...*

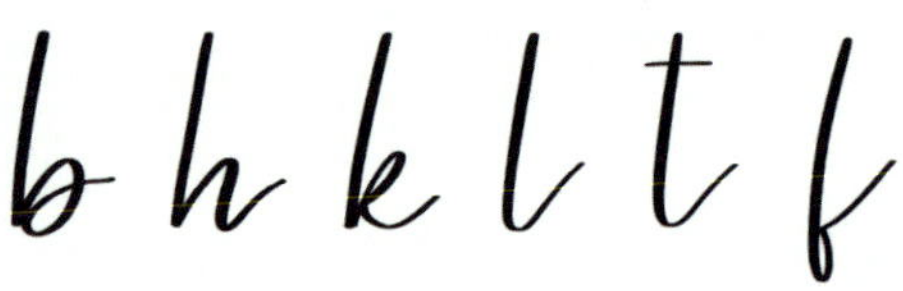

## HERE'S HOW TO DO IT

The letters in this letter group may not appear to have much in common at first glance, but the wrist movement to draw them is a very similar one. For the "e", as in the previous letter group, make sure that you stop after the first upstroke and start again at the same point to finish the letter.

In my view, the "o" has a very special position in hand lettering. The cap in the upper area allows a lot of design freedom. It makes the letter very dominant, artistic and striking. Here, I deliberately drew the downstroke thinly at the top left of the cap, to make the letter look a little more elegant. However, you can also form this area with a typically thicker downstroke.

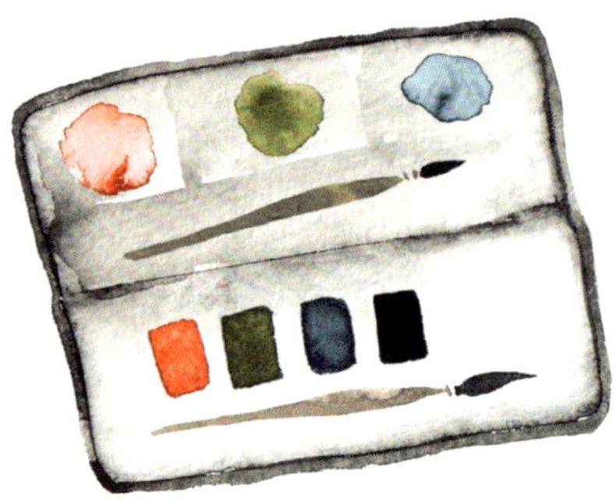

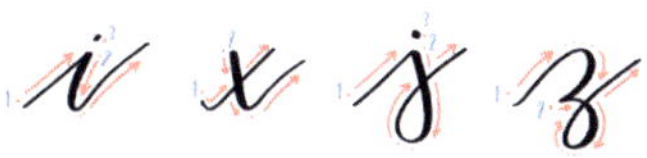

## HERE'S HOW TO DO IT

Always try to extend descenders or loops downwards within your lettering in a similar way. If, for example, with the "g", you decide to draw the downstroke for the descender away to the right, as already described, do the same with letters like "j", as seen here, or "y", as seen in the next letter group. This will give more consistency to your script.

The "z" maybe looks a little difficult – but it consists of only two curves, with the second flowing in a loop as a descender.

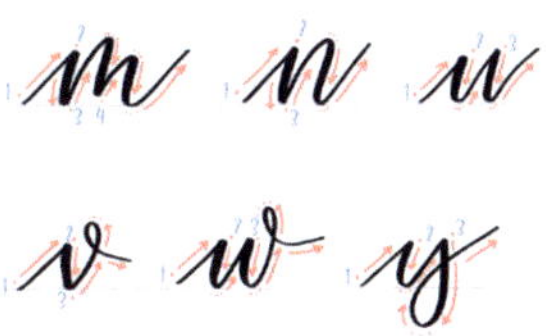

## HERE'S HOW TO DO IT

With the letters "m" and "n", after the first downstroke, put the brush pen back on the lower right point and draw the upstroke away to the right a little again. The result is more white space within the letters (as we saw with "b", "h" and "k").

Try to create additional white space for the letters "u" and "y" by not making them too round and by drawing the second upstroke leaning a little more to the right.

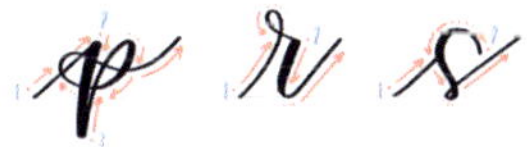

## HERE'S HOW TO DO IT

For the letter "r", make sure you draw the stroke from the first marked point, over the loop to the second marked point and don't remove your brush pen until then. Keep in mind later when lettering words that the route from the previous letter to this second marked point is a little longer. Thinking ahead helps you to carry out this long stroke as cleanly as possible.

You can also vary the size of the loop for the "r" and thus give your lettering a very different appearance.

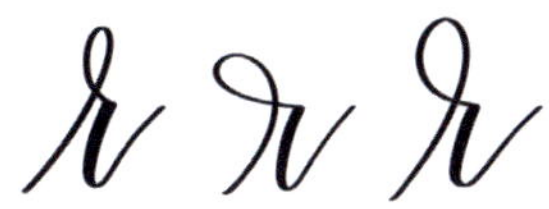

TIP: *All the tips I have given for lettering can be achieved with any pen – it doesn't always have to be a brush pen. For example, you can also implement the stroke you've learned with an ordinary round tip.*

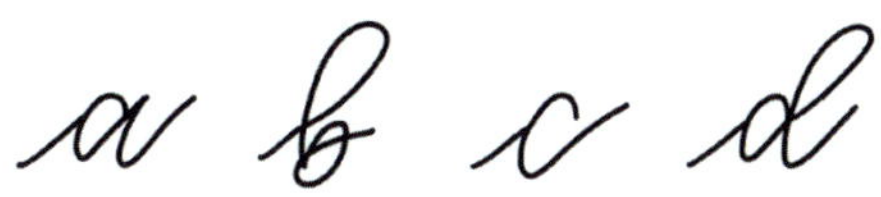

# FAUX CALLIGRAPHY

If you want to keep using the brush lettering effect even with a normal round tip, you can use **faux calligraphy**. This technique is particularly helpful when surfaces, including those other than paper, don't allow for a brush pen. Here are step-by-step instructions to achieve faux calligraphy.

## STEP 1

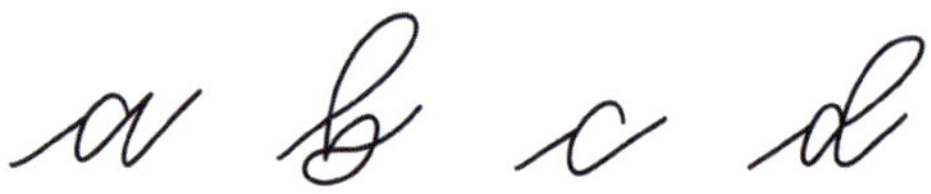

Draw the letters as you learned them in the Practicing Letters section. Use a conventional round tip (no matter what the stroke width) and not a brush pen. Pay special attention to the white spaces within the letters.

## STEP 2

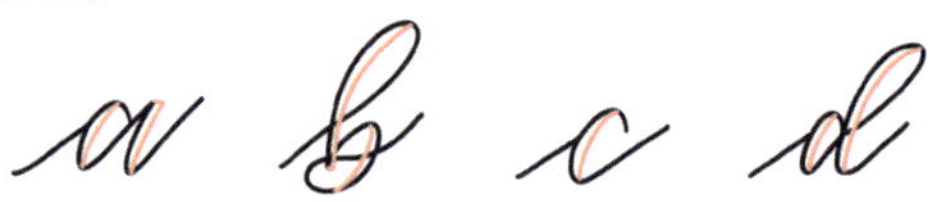

Now your knowledge of downstrokes and upstrokes comes into play: each downstroke is reinforced from top to bottom with a parallel line. In order to have consistency in the script, make sure that the distances between the lines drawn parallel and the original downstroke are the same for each letter. Begin at the apex of a letter (for example, for the "a", start center top) and finish the parallel line at the bottom, also in the center.

## STEP 3

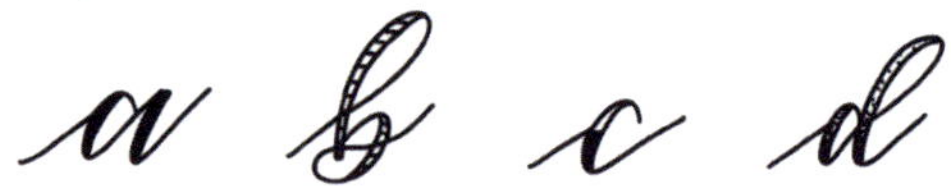

You can paint the resulting gaps completely, fill them with a pattern or simply leave them empty. Decide for yourself which style best suits your respective lettering.

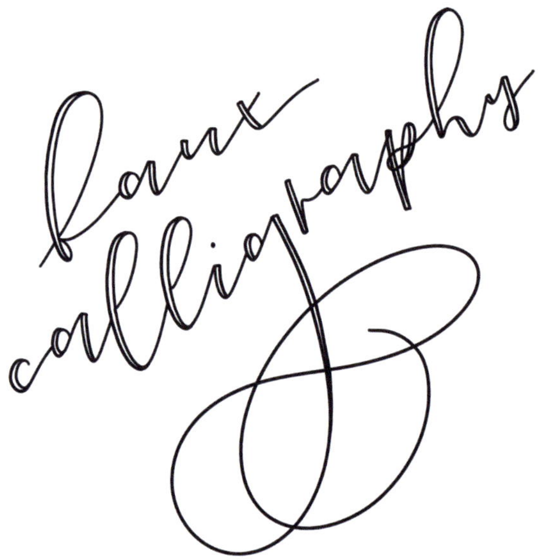

# JOINING UP LETTERS

The secret to the uniform connection of letters is a consistent upstroke in the form of a **connector** – the connection from letter to letter. Be sure to draw all the upstrokes for these joining lines as parallel as possible and to make the gaps as equal as possible with the help of this connector.

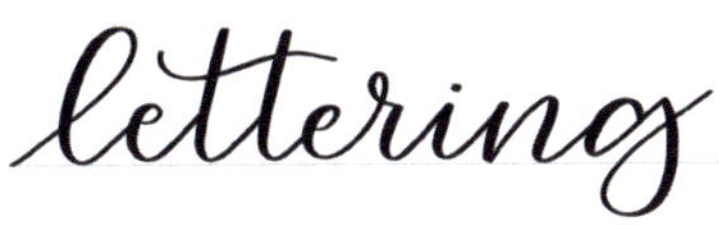


## HERE'S HOW TO DO IT

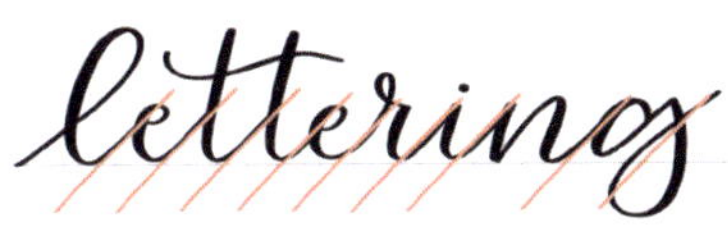


Draw every stroke fully. It doesn't matter if it's in between the letters or at the very end of a word. To ensure precise lettering, place each stroke consciously and don't let the connectors "bleed" with momentum.

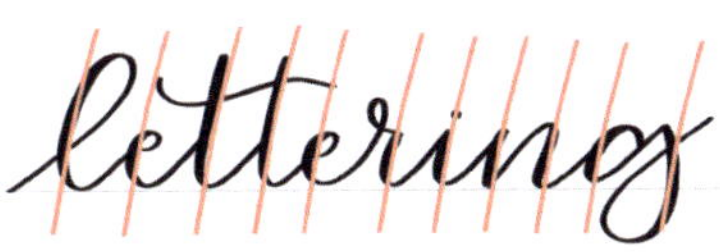


For the lettering of a word, also pay attention to an even **angle of inclination** for all downstrokes that you draw within the letters. By forming them as parallel as possible, you can create an even more harmonious script.

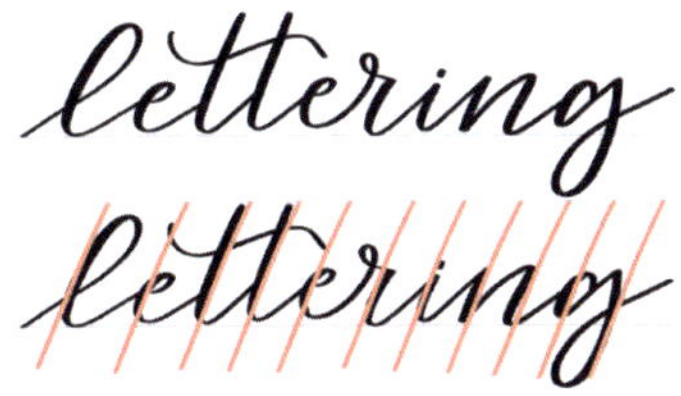


You can determine the angle of inclination yourself. Whether you want to drag every downstroke vertically from the top down, or to make your lettering a little more italic (i.e. tilted to the right) is entirely up to you. If you've chosen an angle of inclination for your downstrokes, stay with it as much as possible.

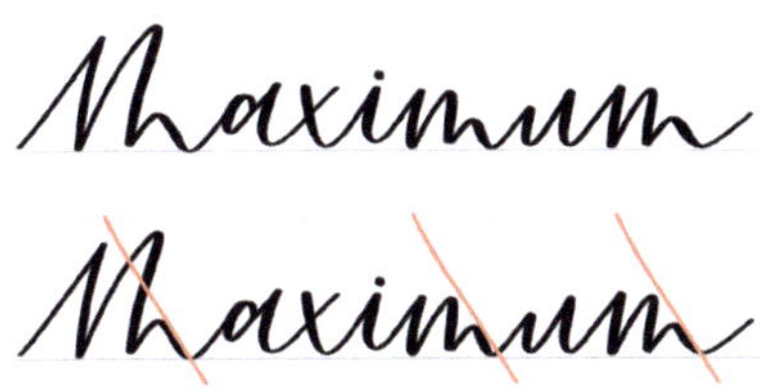


Having said that you should try to maintain an even angle of inclination for all downstrokes, you can break this rule of thumb in deliberately selected places if you feel comfortable doing so and if you can still create a harmonious script. So, with selected letters, you can **change direction** with the downstroke, drawing the angle of inclination in the opposite direction. **N.B.** This opposite placing of the downstroke doesn't work for every letter and it won't suit all lettering. Never forget that readability is always the top priority.

## BOUNCE LETTERING

In order to create a loose "dancing" script, don't sit the letters strictly on the baseline, as they have been until now, but go further beyond it. Start by trying to pull the downstrokes at the end of certain letters a little further down. Don't make the length of these downstrokes too uniform, but vary them somewhat from letter to letter, so that there is a certain degree of balance within a word.

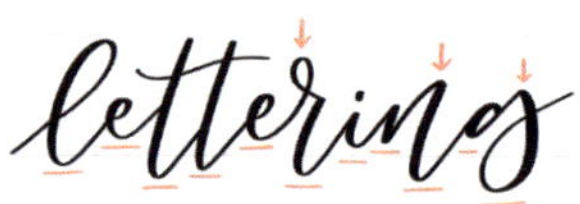


TIP: *In Alphabet 2: Bouncy Brush Script, the letters you can "dance" using extended downstrokes are marked. Any letters without markings are less suitable for this technique. You can vary the letters in different ways for more balance in your bounce lettering; for example, you can draw the size of the vowels smaller and raise them slightly from the baseline, or make them taller. Likewise, you can pull up other parts of the letters further than usual, such as, for example, the loop of the "r" and the "w" or the so-called shoulders of the "m" and "n".*

## THE GRID LINE

Until now, all hand-lettered letters and words were sitting on a grid line. This grid is composed as shown in this diagram:

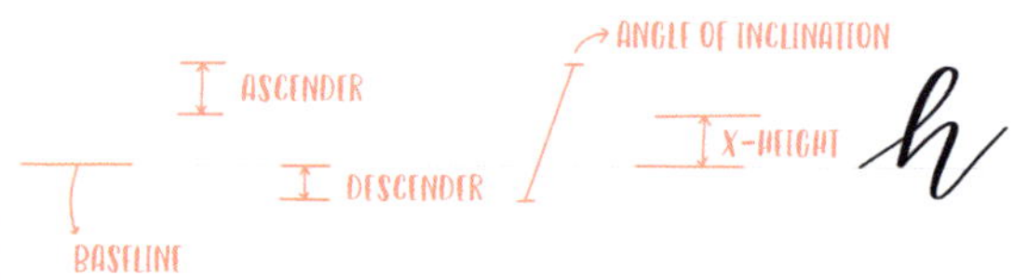


You can vary certain types of script yourself by simply pushing the x-height up or down. With this trick, you can give your lettering a completely different feel and make it part of your unique style.

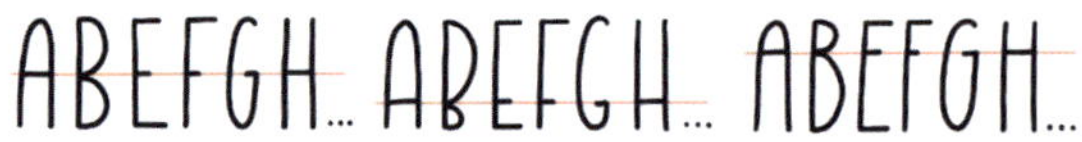


The seven alphabets on the following pages in different types and styles of script are intended to serve as a source of inspiration and to help you practice.

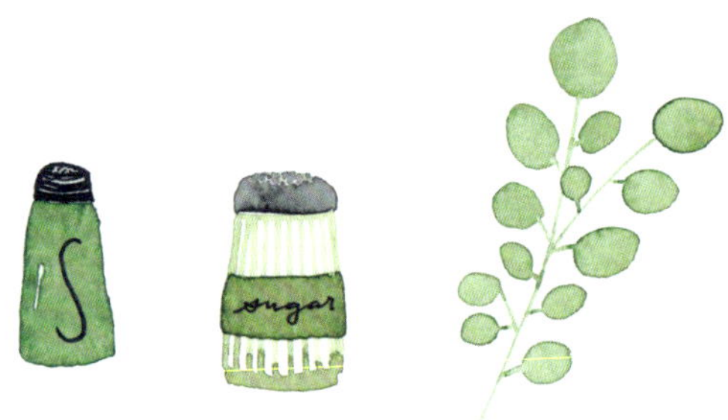

## ALPHABET 1: BRUSH SCRIPT

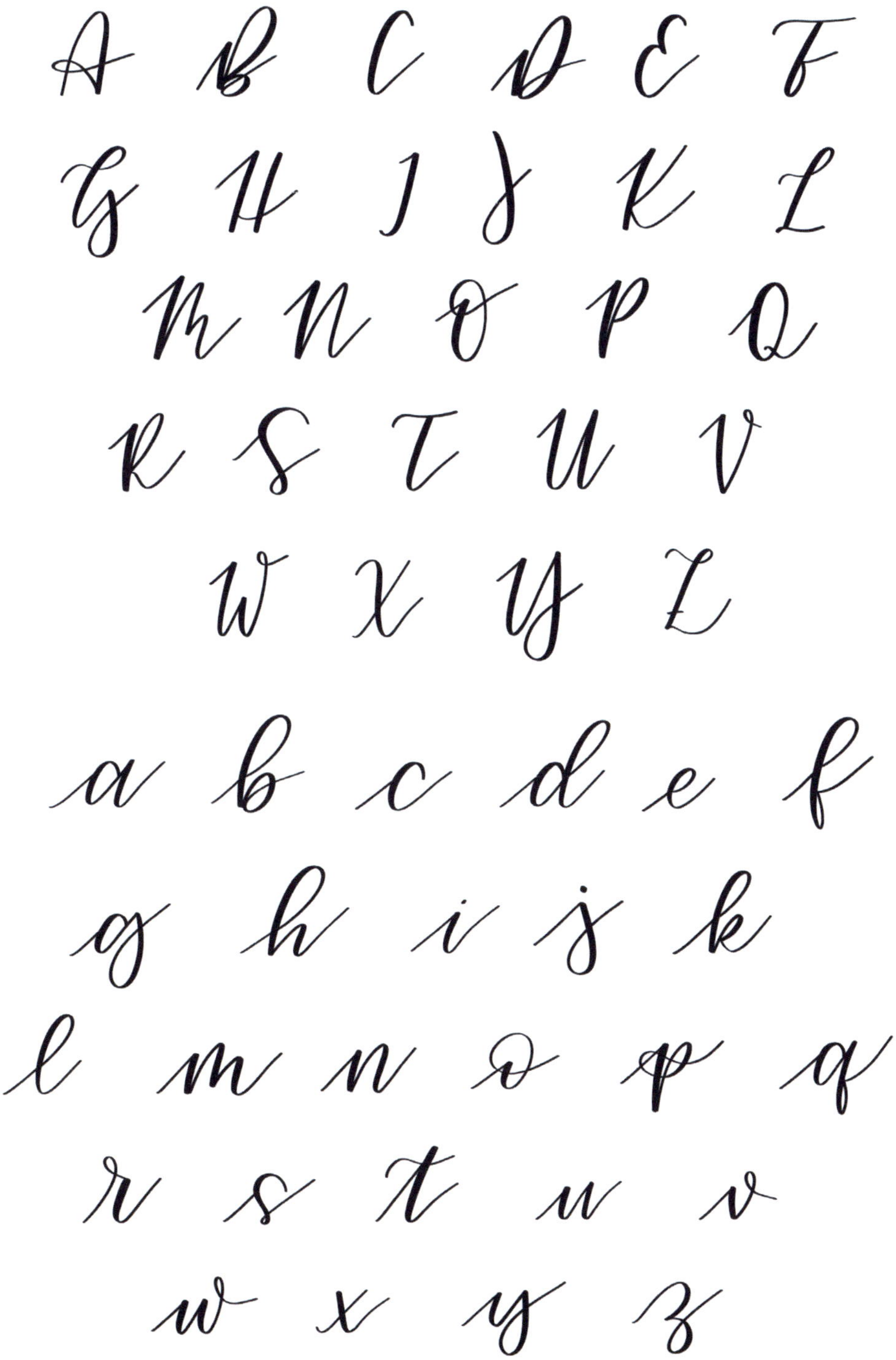

## ALPHABET 2: BOUNCY BRUSH SCRIPT

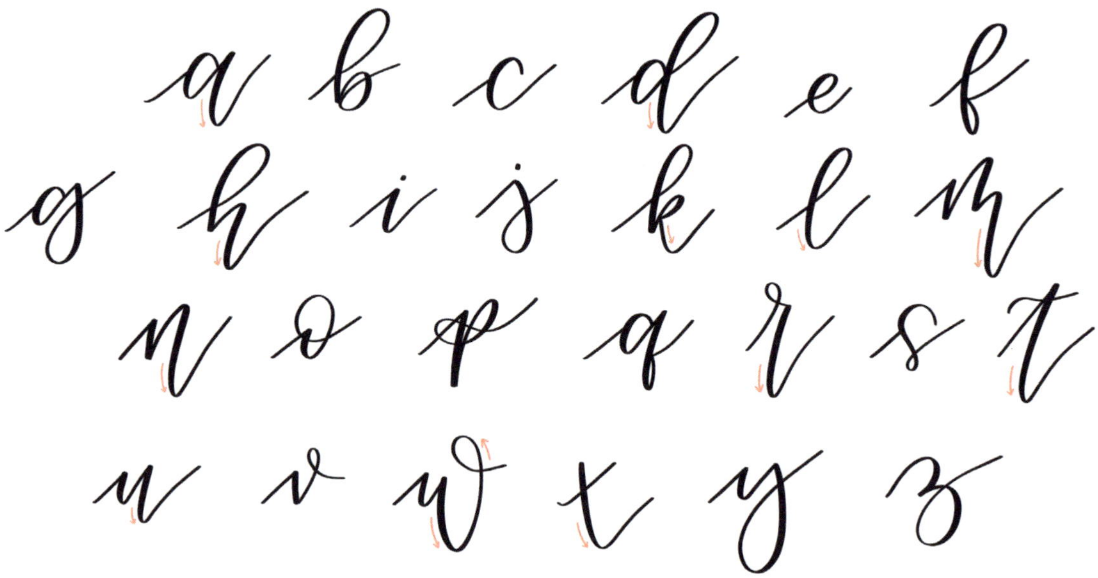

## ALPHABET 3: MONOLINE

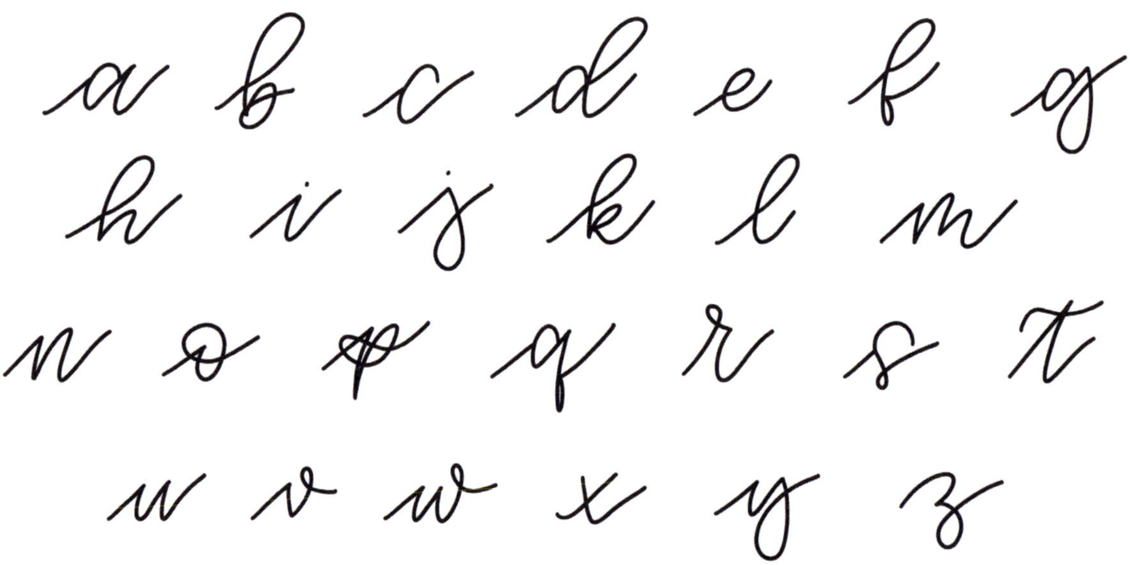

## ALPHABET 4: FAUX CALLIGRAPHY

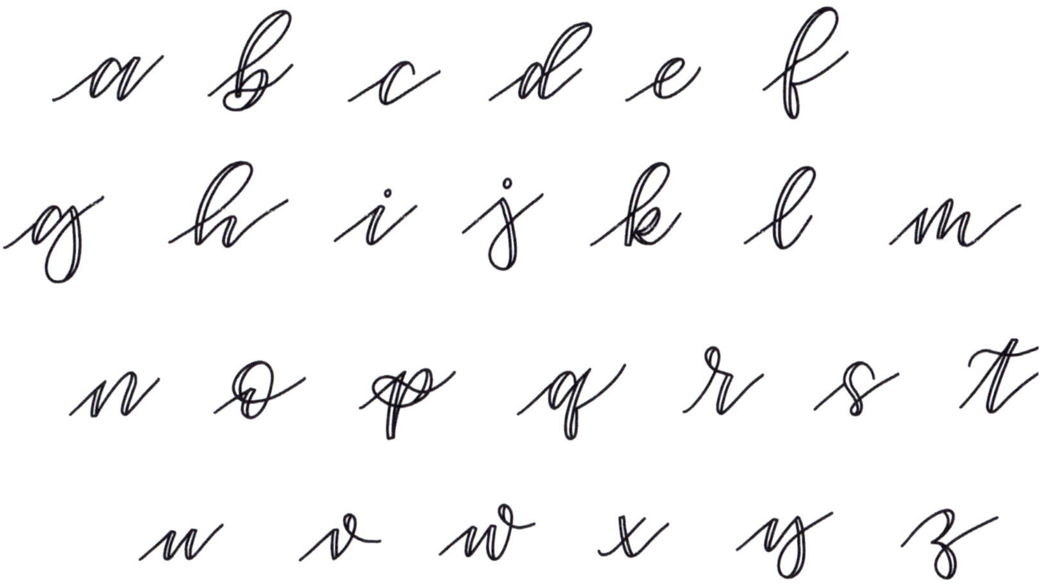

## ALPHABET 5: EXTENDED SCRIPT

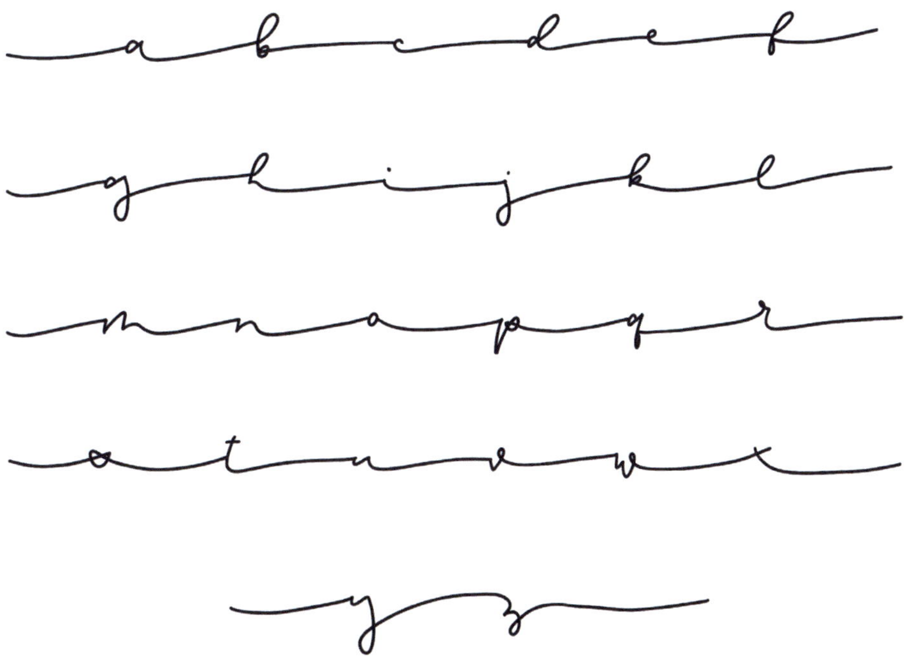

## ALPHABET 6: SANS SERIF (NARROW)

A B C D E F G H

I J K L M N O P

Q R S T U V W X Y Z

## ALPHABET 7: BRUSH SERIF

A B C D E F G H I J

K L M N O P Q R

S T U V W X Y Z

# Watercolor Know-How

In this chapter, I'll show you the basics of watercolor technique, introduce you to interesting facts about color, and explore with you the characteristics of watercolor paint (with a look at gouache, too!). My aim is to instruct and inspire you to create your own personal color palettes for each project.

## CHECKLIST

### WHAT YOU NEED

- [ ] Watercolor paint
- [ ] Watercolor brush
- [ ] Watercolor paper
- [ ] Two water containers (for dirty water and clean water)
- [ ] Cleaning cloth or kitchen roll (for blotting the brush)
- [ ] Mixing area (in your paint box, separate mixing palette, or another smooth surface such as an old plate)

## PAINT-TO-WATER MIXING RATIO

Before I show you different watercolor techniques, it's important that you get a feeling for the mixing ratio of paint to water. There isn't just one mixing ratio; it will depend greatly on how you want to create your watercolor project and your personal preference for the painting process. In addition, the paper itself has a big influence on the paint-to-water mixing ratio you work with.

TIP: *The more water you add to the paint, the higher the transparency. Equally, if more paint is added, the color becomes more opaque. Try it out for yourself!*

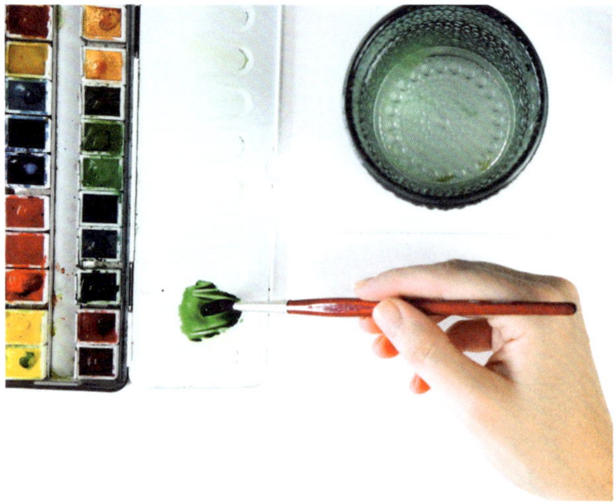

### STEP 1

Thoroughly wet your watercolor brush in one of the water containers and activate your chosen paint with circular movements in your paint box. You now have paint pigments on your brush that you can apply to your mixing surface. Dip the brush briefly into the water again and mix the water absorbed by the bristles with it, without washing out the brush. If there is still too little paint on the mixing surface, repeat this process.

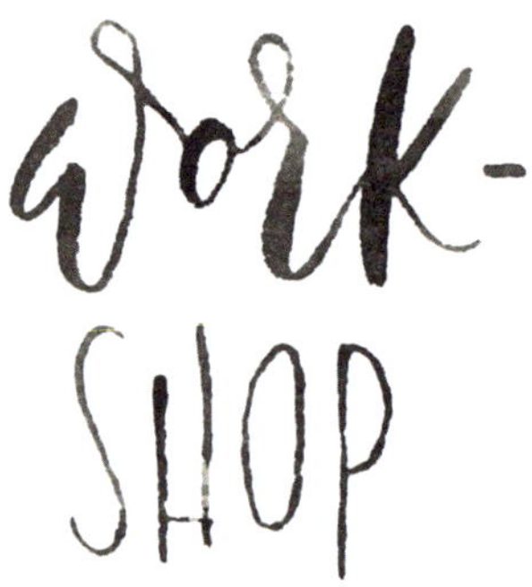


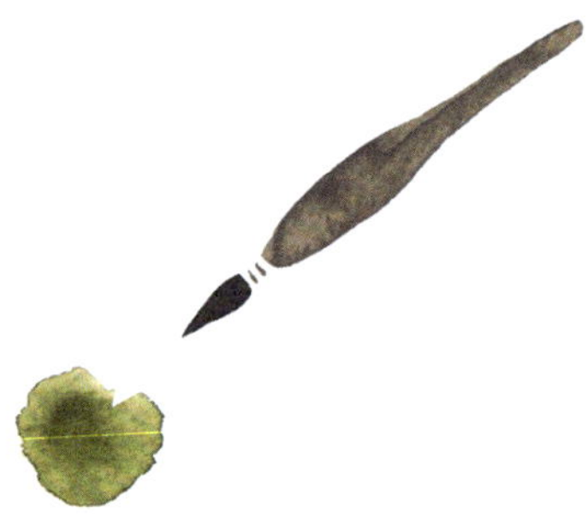

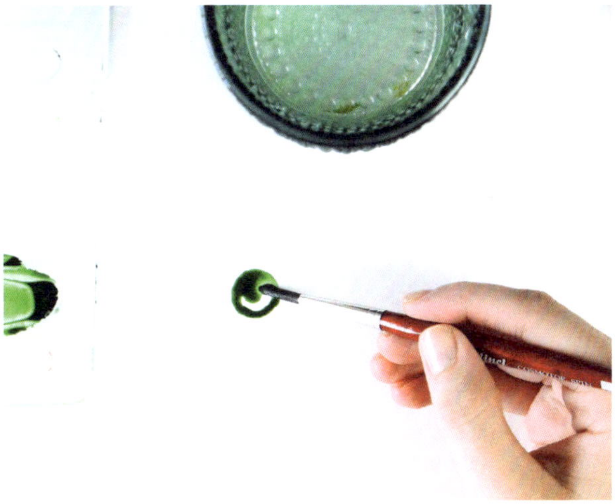

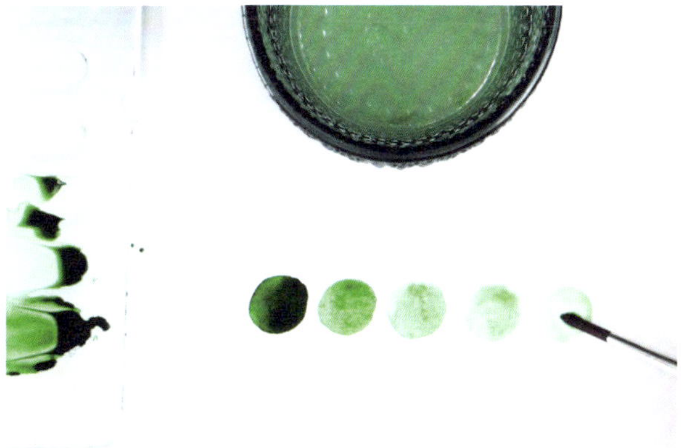

## STEP 2

You should now have a good starting point for testing the desired paint-to-water mixing ratio. Paint a rectangle or circle on the watercolor paper with the diluted paint. As your brush still holds enough watercolor paint, you don't need to dip it into the paint area again. Instead, just dip the brush tip very briefly into the water, then wipe off the excess water and immediately paint the second area of color alongside the first.

## STEP 3

Repeat this process and try to put three to five areas of color on the paper. Let the areas dry and see how the transparency of the paint behaves on the paper you're using. Do this with all the colors you want to use for your respective watercolor project. This is the best way to decide which paint-to-water mixing ratio you want to work with per shade.

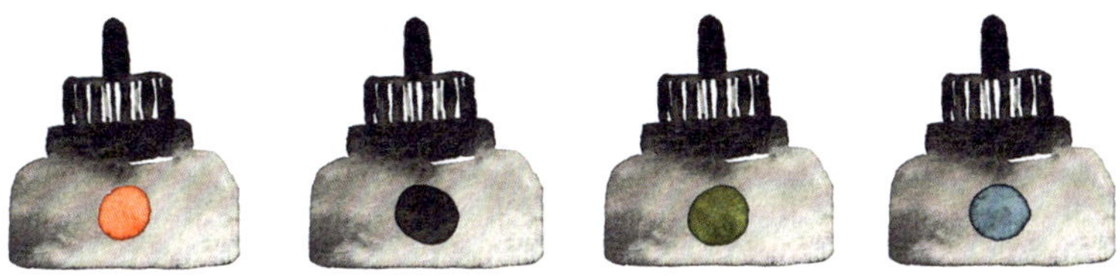

# BASIC TECHNIQUES

## WASHING

Washing is a technique that allows you to create seamless watercolor gradients either over large areas or within specific areas.

### HERE'S HOW TO DO IT

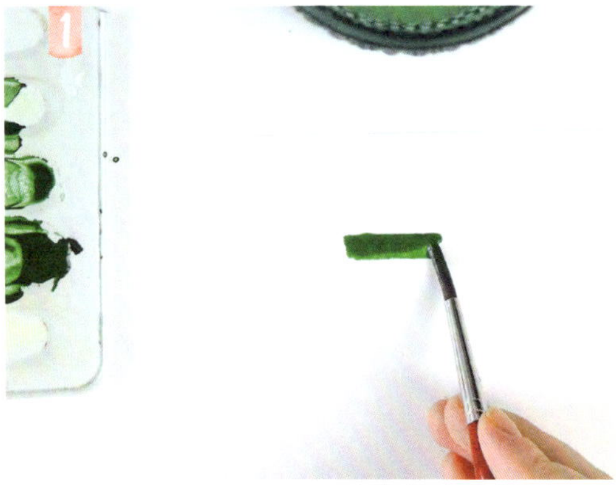


Paint an area on the watercolor paper. Wash the brush out well afterwards – preferably in the clean water container.

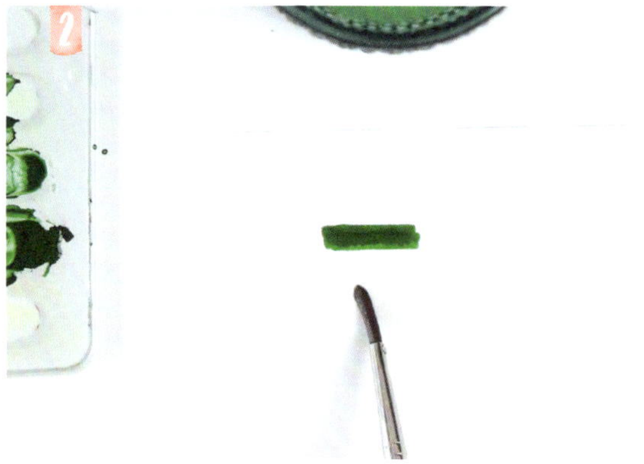


Now start from the other side, from below in my example, to prime an area with clean water up to the painted area.

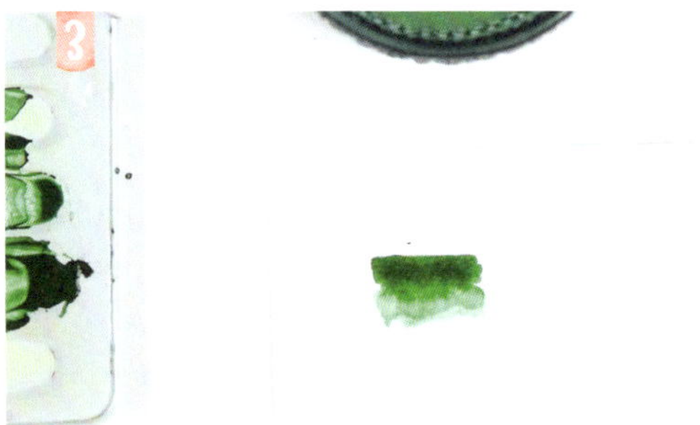


At the point where the brush touches the painted area, the paint runs and passes seamlessly over the wet area.

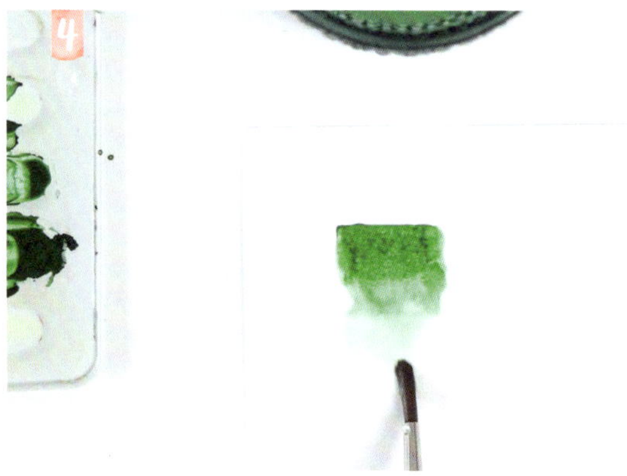


You can then control the gradient a little by shaping it with the washed, clean brush.

## GLAZING

Glazing is done in layers. The paint areas that have already dried shine through (depending on the color selection) and result in new color nuances in the overlapping areas. Use different colors to enhance the effect.

### HERE'S HOW TO DO IT

1

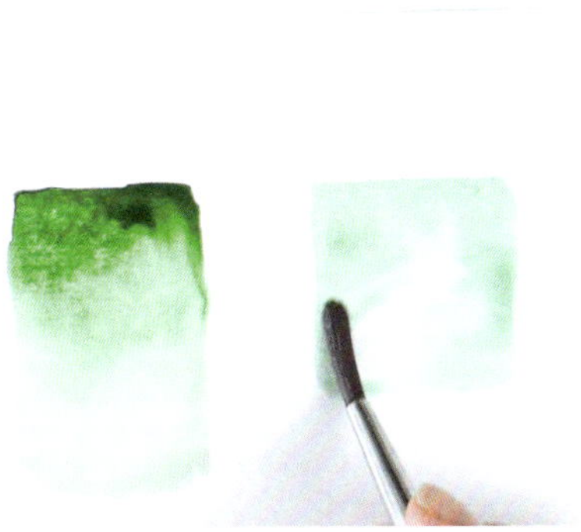

Paint an area of color with a high water content, i.e. as transparent as possible. Let the area dry well.

2

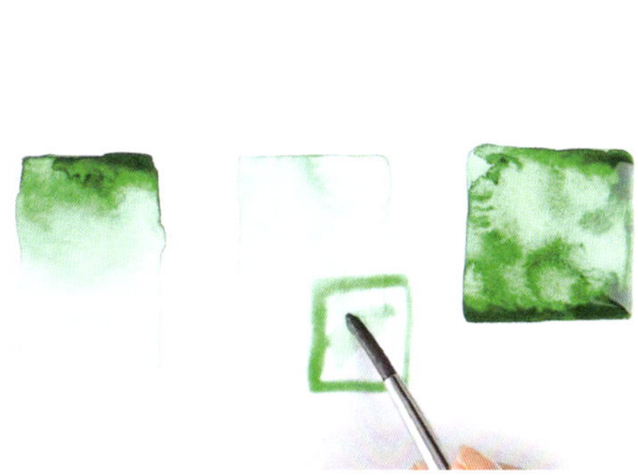

Now add a second area of color, also as transparent as possible, which overlaps with the first area in some places.

3

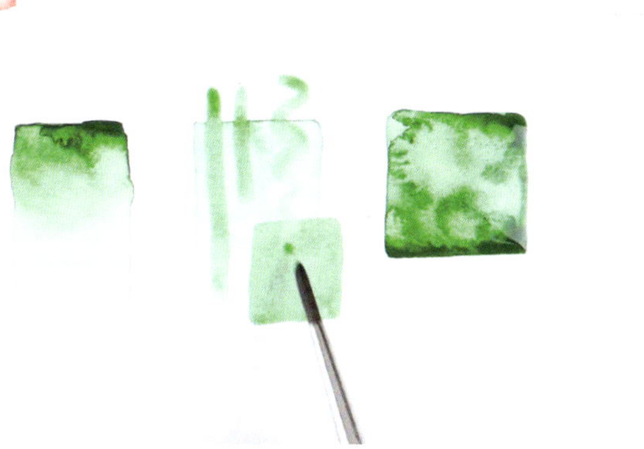

Always let the respective layers dry well before adding further layers.

TIP: *Always work from light to dark with watercolor paints, particularly when you work in layers. Plan in white spaces too, i.e. blank (paper) areas, from the start. It's virtually impossible to lighten them up again afterwards.*

## WET-ON-WET

The wet-on-wet technique is probably the most well-known of the three basic techniques. It's a matter of priming an area either with clean water or with some paint and continuing to work in a wet state.

### HERE'S HOW TO DO IT

1

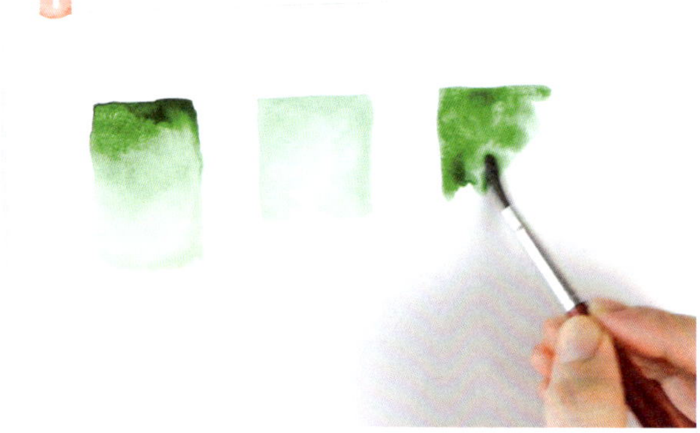

Prime either an area of paint or one of clean water, making sure the entire area is wet, in preparation for selectively adding paint to it.

2

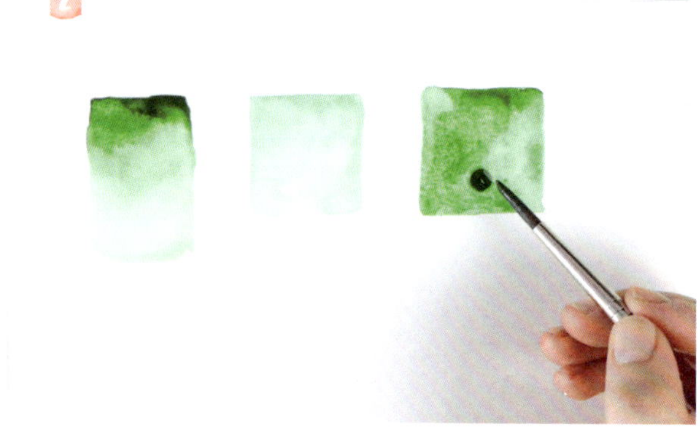

On a very wet surface, dabbed-on paint tends to remain where it is placed. If the primed surface is a little less wet, the new paint can be spread a little more.

3

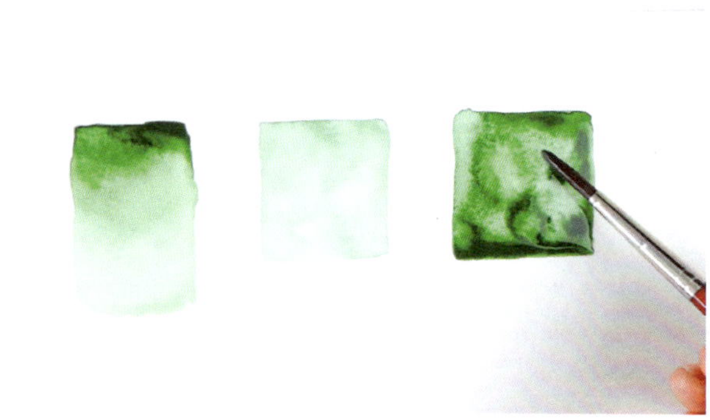

Instead of using additional paint, you can also tap or sprinkle over clean water. Carefully soak up excess water with a piece of kitchen roll.

TIP: *You can sprinkle watercolor paint by wetting your brush well with water and paint, holding the brush over your watercolor paper and tapping the brush with the index finger of your other hand.*

# HANDLING THE BRUSH

## BRUSH EXERCISES

To help you master your most important tool when illustrating with watercolor, start each watercolor session with a few warm-up exercises. Take advantage of the round tip to be able to paint very thin lines, as well as wide ones. Pictured here are some brush exercises that you can try as a warm-up.

For these warm-up exercises, I used the da Vinci series 488 wash brush, size 0 (Spin-Synthetics).

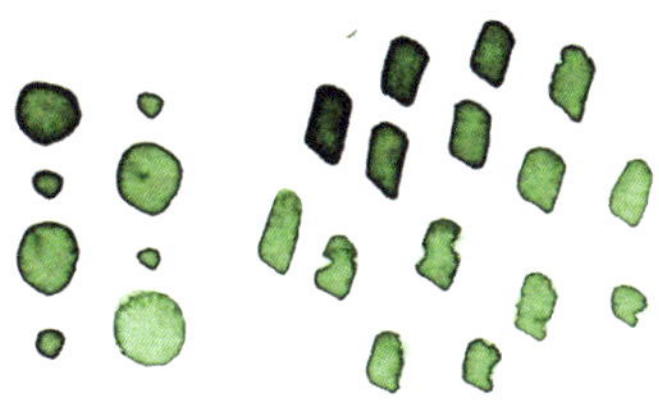

## TIPS FOR BRUSH CARE

To give your brushes as long a lifespan as possible, it's essential to wash them with lukewarm water after use. As watercolor paint is already water-soluble to a high degree, this is the simplest and gentlest way to care for your brushes. Don't leave your brushes in the water container, otherwise they may lose their shape. It's best to lay your brushes horizontally to dry before you put them away.

Once you've washed out your round or wash brush with water, carefully shape the tip of the bristles back to a point by letting the brush slide through your thumb and index finger while slightly turning it. That way you'll ensure that your brush will keep its shape for a long time.

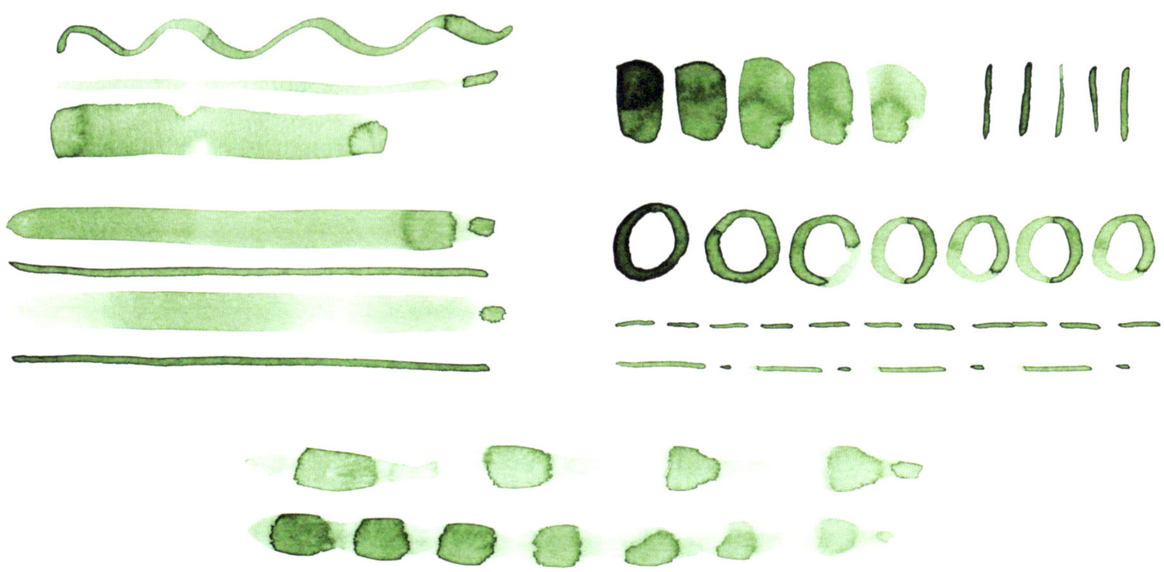

# COLOR KNOWLEDGE

I've deliberately not called this section "color theory" because, personally, I find that term quite daunting. It kept me from immersing myself in the world of (watercolor) paints and color combinations for far too long. What I'd like to give you at this point are so-called "color harmonies" to prepare you for preparing your personal color palette.

If you want to try out new color combinations but you aren't quite sure which colors might go together, you can stick to these generally applicable color harmonies as a first step. You'll find the **color wheel** (according to Johannes Itten) helpful. I've summarized some well-known color harmonies here.

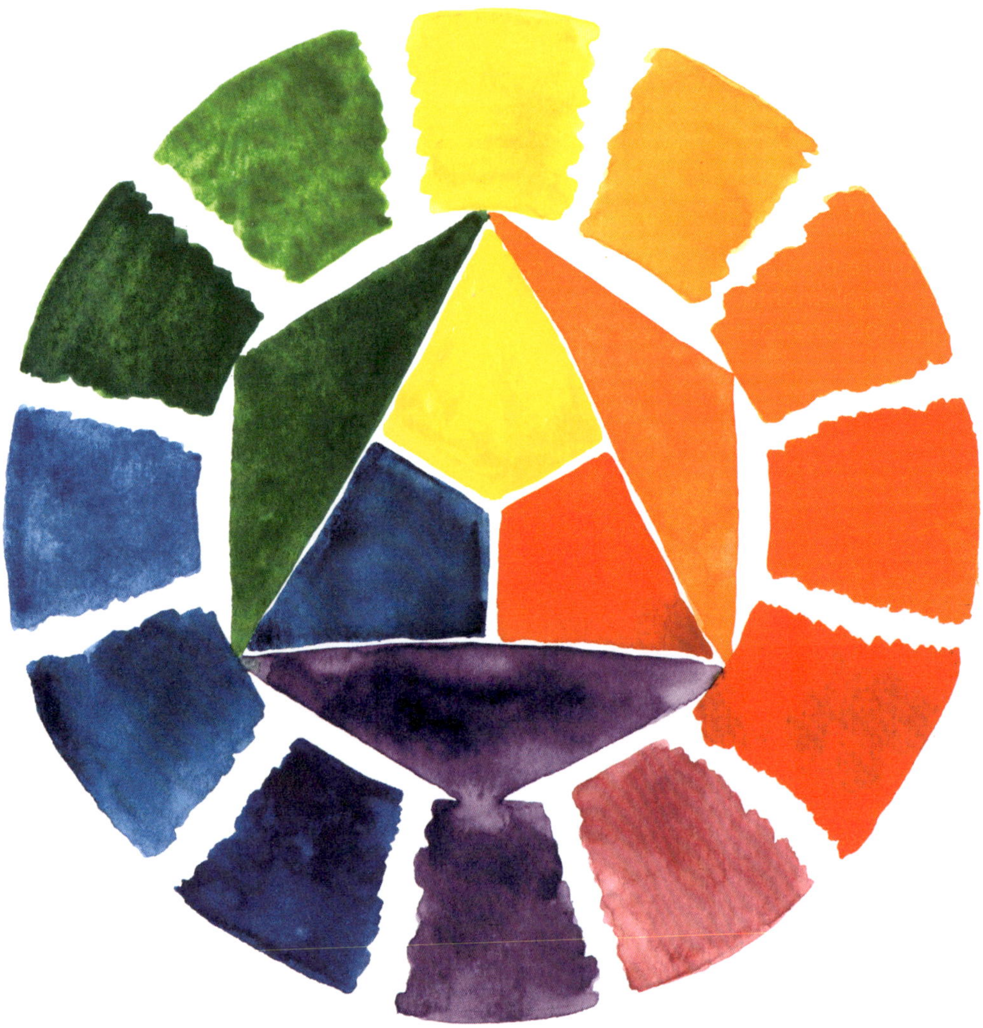

## COMPLEMENTARY COLORS

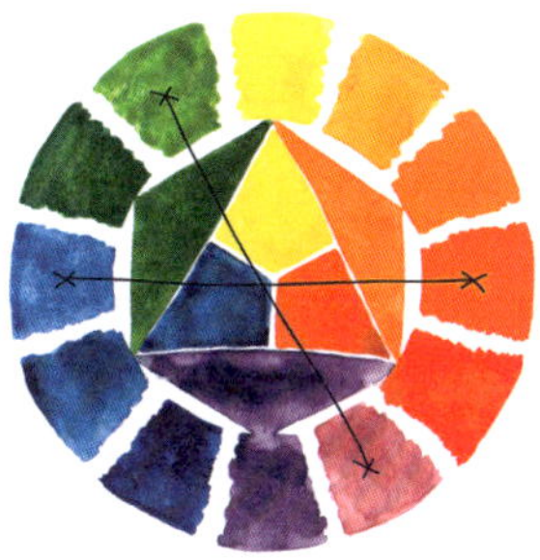

Colors that lie directly **opposite** each other on the color wheel are referred to as complementary colors and are generally considered to be harmonious. However, if you mix complementary colors with each other, you won't achieve a bright, new shade, you'll just make the color darker. For example, if you want to mix a blue a little darker, you can also use the complementary color orange for darkening instead of another dark color.

## SQUARE COLORS

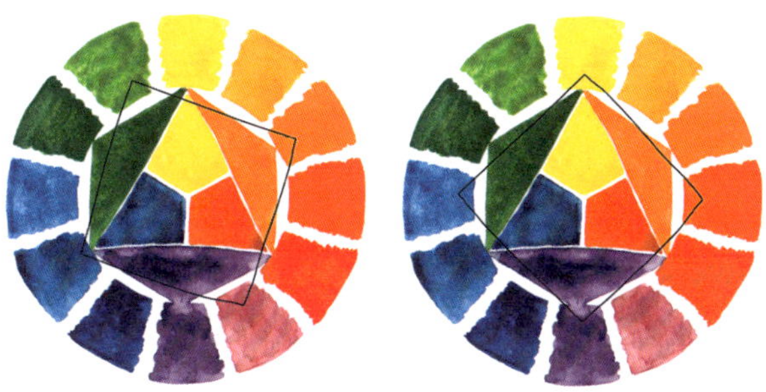

Square colors are created when a **square** is drawn within the wheel. The color fields touched by the corners of the square are also classified as harmonious.

## TRIAD COLORS

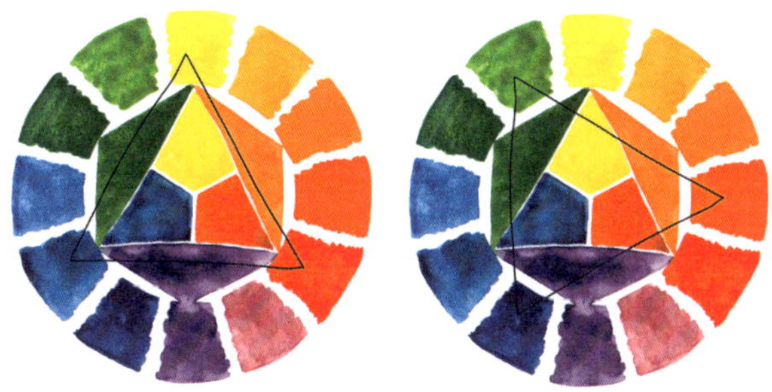

A harmonious triad color scheme arises through an **equilateral triangle** within the color wheel. You can mentally rotate this triangle to explore and try out new color combinations.

## ANALOGOUS COLORS

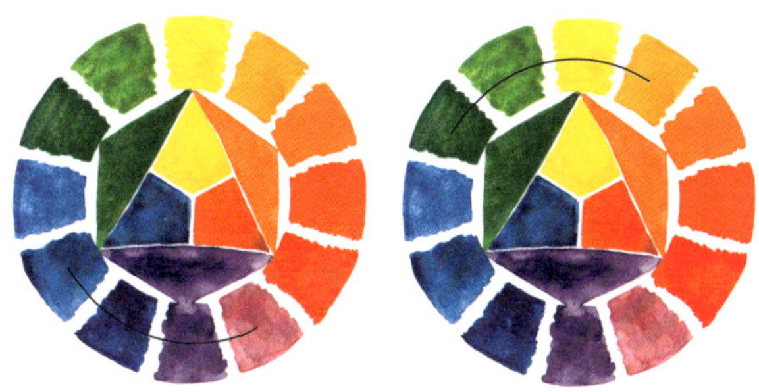

The three to four color fields that lie directly next to each other on the color wheel are also considered harmonious.

Knowledge of such color harmonies will help you when putting together a color palette, but the possibilities for the final color selection within the selected color fields are still almost endless. For example, you can change colors selected from the color wheel by making them look warmer or colder. Green towards yellow tends to be warmer than green towards blue. In addition, you can discover new color nuances by applying your knowledge of tonal range, transparency and opacity, and I'd like to share this knowledge with you in the next section of this chapter.

TIP: *You can mix any color with the primary colors red, yellow or blue and discover new color variations in this way.* **N.B.** *The more colors you mix, the more likely you'll be to get a solid brown as a result. Therefore, when mixing colors, focus on a maximum of two to three colors.*

## MIXING PRIMARY COLORS

In the example below, I've mixed the secondary colors (green, violet and orange) with the primary colors (red, yellow and blue). You can see that complementary colors (using the example of violet and yellow, as well as orange and blue) in equal proportions are less suitable for mixing. However, if you only want to darken a color a little using the complementary color, add a little less of the color. Using the example of green and red, you can see that adding only a little bit of red results in a darker green. If I had mixed red and green in equal parts, the result would have been a dark brown. Overall, these examples show you how you can achieve new, strong shades by adding primary colors. This works not just with secondary colors, but with all colors directly from the tube or the watercolor pan.

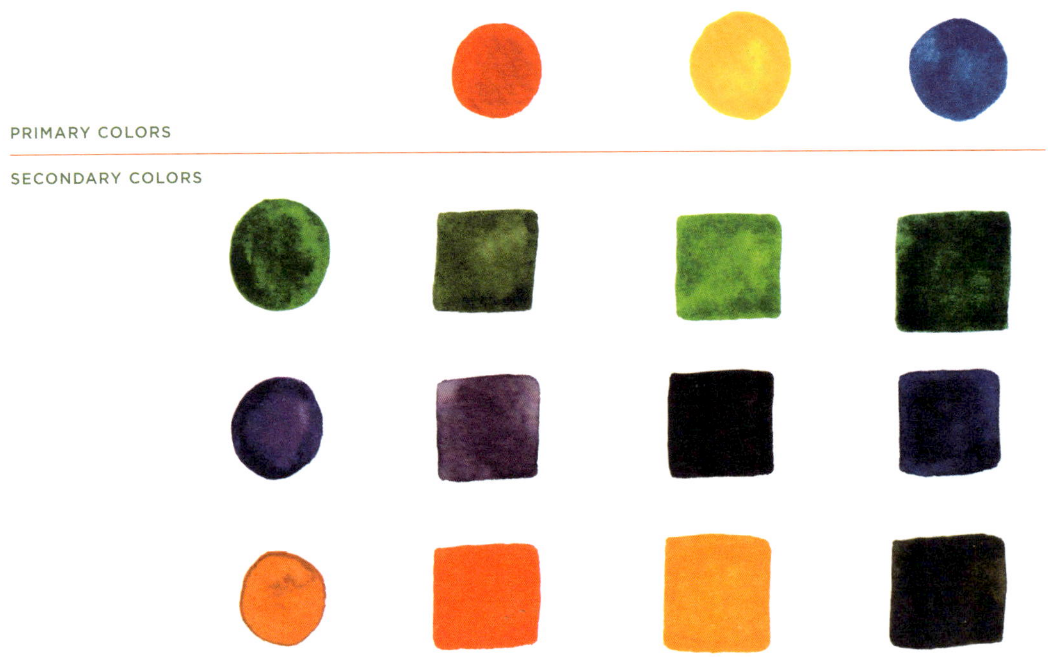

# TONAL RANGE, TRANSPARENCY, OPACITY

The **tonal range** describes the gradation of a shade between very dark and very light. The strength of color or intensity of the color changes depending on the gradation of the tonal range.

You can basically lighten colors with white watercolor paint. However, this **lightening** with white not only results in a lighter shade, but also a more pastel effect, and in most cases, more opacity. Lightening with water is also possible. However, keep in mind that this kind of lightening increases the transparency of the color.

You can basically **darken** any color with black. However, I recommend that you use gray tones. For one thing, it's often harder to use the right amount of black. Also, the danger of using black is that the darkened color looks dirty quickly. Personally, I like to darken colors with earth colors, e.g. brown or dark green, or to use a darker tone of the same color.

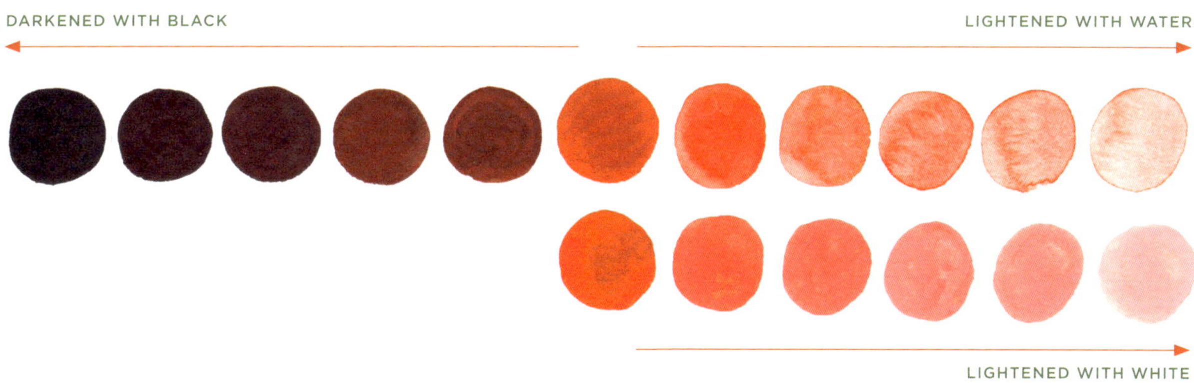

# YOUR PERSONAL COLOR PALETTE

You now know a bit about the interaction of colors in relation to the well-known color harmonies and you also know a few tips and tricks for mixing, lightening and darkening. Now it's time to dedicate yourself to your personal color palette. You can put together new, individual color palettes for each piece of work; or you can adjust a repertoire of colors that can be found in all your pieces.

## STEP 1

Using the color wheel from the Color Knowledge section, think about which color should fundamentally dominate your color palette. Is it more of a warmer color, such as orange or red, or would a colder color, such as a shade of blue, stand out? Which **starting color** do you generally feel most comfortable with or works best with your chosen design? So, first choose a color – it's the starting point for your personal color palette.

TIP: *You can start by adjusting your color palette digitally (using Photoshop, Procreate or another program) and only afterwards try to mix these shades with watercolor paint. While this method usually saves on paint, it does require knowledge in advance about mixing colors.*

## STEP 2

Now go through the color harmonies described in Color Knowledge and consider whether this results in an initial **color combination** (with two to three other colors) that appeals to you. If not, you can create your own color card with all your watercolor shades. Your aim is to decide on two or three matching colors in addition to your chosen starting color.

## STEP 3

You now have a total of three to four colors, which are your basis for further selection. Experiment in this step with the selected watercolor paints and see how the colors with high transparency and high opacity look on watercolor paper when dried. Also, try to darken and lighten each color, as described in Tonal Range, Transparency, Opacity, creating new shades and nuances. Try mixing your original colors with the three primary colors (red, yellow and blue); you'll be surprised by the shades created.

TIP: *Note on each paint area, what colors you've added, how you've lightened them or what colors you've darkened them with, as a record to remix them later as required.*

## STEP 4

Your three to four original colors have now been transformed into a rich color palette. In this step, this color palette is your decision-making tool as to which shades you'll finally put together into your personal or project-related color palette. Choose a maximum of **three main colors**, which should dominate your work, and a maximum of **three highlight colors**, which you'll use to help with the details, and for smaller areas, etc.

TIP: *If your own color palette is not based on the color harmonies described or other color knowledge, that's fine. Ultimately, not everything we find harmonious needs to be explained.*

# AN INTRODUCTION TO GOUACHE

Gouache paint is very similar in its use to watercolor paint, but there are differences. While gouache is also a water-soluble paint, it has a much higher pigmentation and therefore also opacity.

In principle, you can use gouache like watercolor paint. For example, it can also be easily reactivated with water on a color palette (or on paper) after drying. The main difference between gouache and watercolor paint is that gouache has a much higher opacity and dries with a matte appearance. The most difficult thing about painting with gouache is probably the paint-to-water mixing ratio. Try to make the paint as creamy as possible by adding just a little water. That way, you're able to achieve clear contours and edges, while retaining the paint's opacity.

For some projects, I have used gouache paint for highlights on my watercolor designs, but for other projects, e.g. Green & Floral: Floral Greeting and several of the Insects projects (Beetle Canvases, A Bug's Life and Moth Notebook Cover), I have used just gouache. You can also paint all the projects in this book exclusively with watercolor paint, of course.

Maybe gouache will inspire you, as it did me, and you'd like to experiment with it when you're more confident with the watercolor basics – I hope I can encourage you with one of the projects in this book.

TIP: *A few manufacturers also offer acrylic gouache. Acrylic gouache resembles conventional gouache paint in its handling and in the painting process. However, there is a serious difference: if the paint is dry, it can no longer be reactivated or dissolved. When painting on materials other than paper, this results in far greater project possibilities. When using it, however, you should be careful to have as little paint as possible on your mixing palette, as it dries relatively quickly and can no longer be used afterwards.*

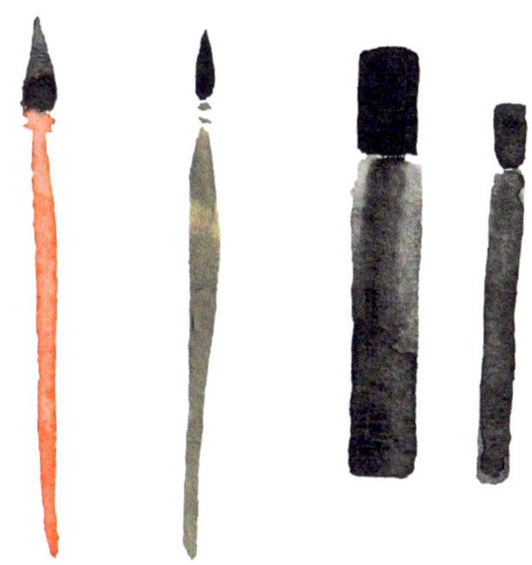

# PROJECTS

With this colorful variety of designs, I'd like to encourage you to tackle your own individual hand lettering and illustration projects. There are five subject categories, from abstract to insects. The projects are divided into three levels of difficulty, which is indicated by the number of pen holders. One pen holder means simple, two medium difficulty and three difficult. But don't worry: each of the projects is easy to do – some just require a little more practice.

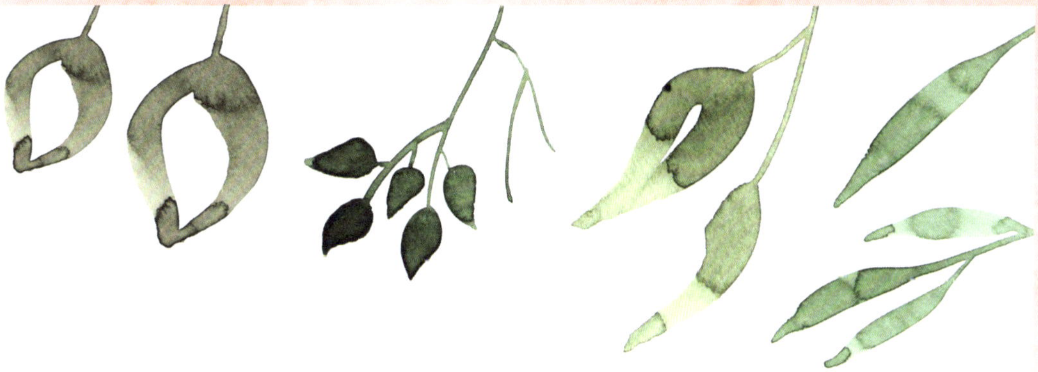

Peace begins with a Smile

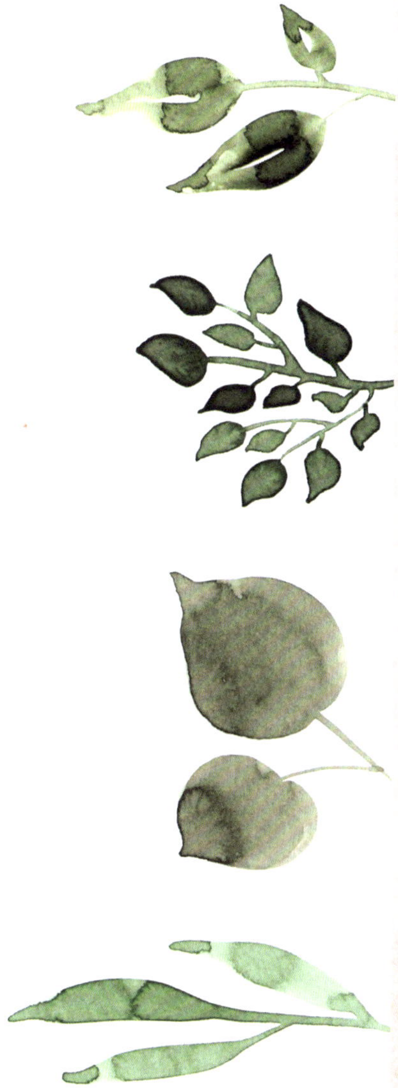

## PROJECTS

# Moodboard

A moodboard helps you to experiment with selected colors and to get a better feeling for the paint-to-water mixing ratio, depending on the color chosen and the brush and paper used.

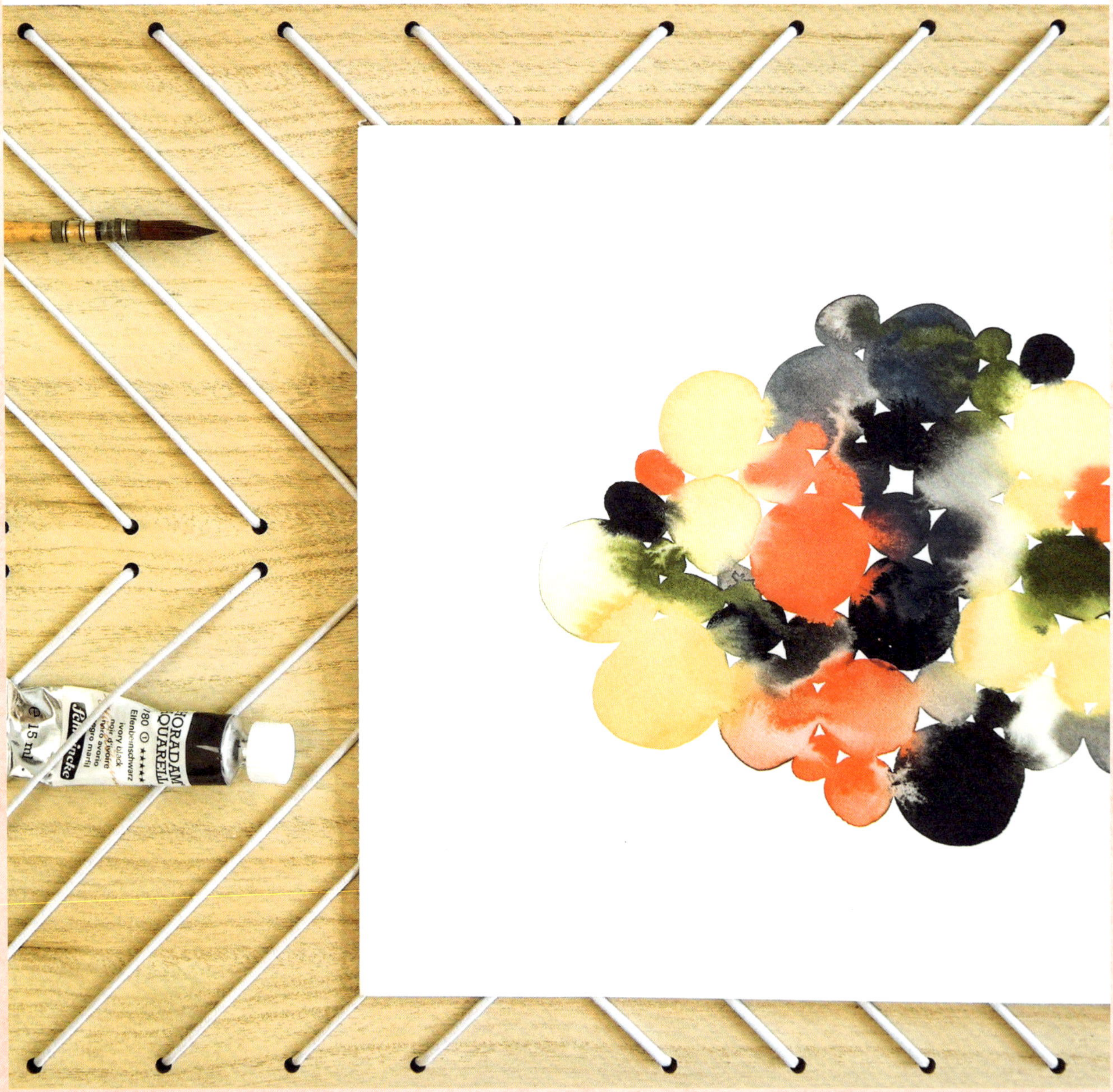

## MATERIALS

- Watercolor paper
- Watercolor paint
- Watercolor brush

TIP: *Try out a wash brush, which is different to a conventional round brush both in the painting process and in the result.*

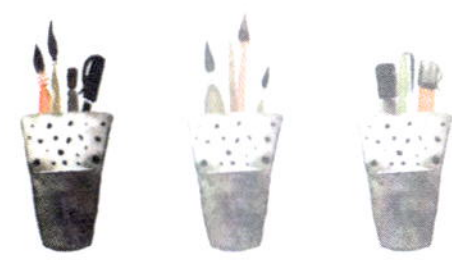

## Here's how to do it

1. Start the abstract moodboard by painting your first circle. Make absolutely sure that your work is wet enough, so that you can subsequently run the paint into other areas.

2. Now paint the second circle (either in the same color or choose another) and let the two shapes touch each other at one point. The edge of the first shape thus touches the edge of the second shape – but they don't overlap. You don't have to make perfectly shaped circles. You can adjust the shape and size as you choose, and you can decide spontaneously which color, size and position you'll give to the next area.

3. Repeat these steps until you feel satisfied with the arrangement and quantity of shapes.

4. Let your moodboard dry well. Try to reflect on it briefly afterwards: look to see whether you find the color placement harmonious, and ask yourself how the dried colors work together. If the result is harmonious in your view, you can use the moodboard for other (illustration) purposes and watercolor projects. If not, think about which colors may seem too dominant, which colors would benefit from more space between them, and even which colors interfere with, rather than support, the interaction.

1

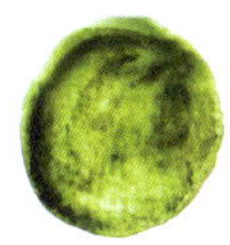

2

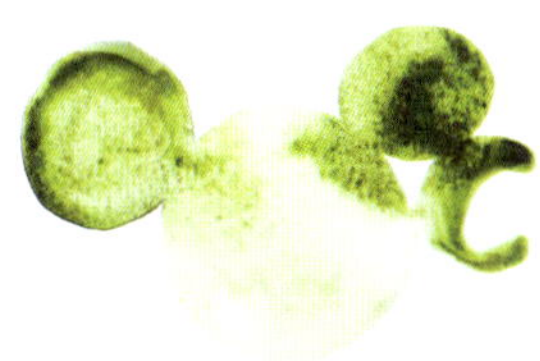

3

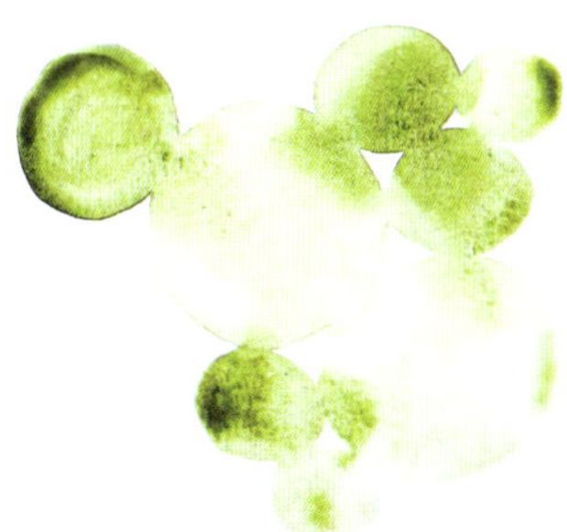

# Inspiration Cards

Inspiration cards can be like balm for the soul. For this project, experiment with the shape of the brush, test out colors on their own and see how they interact, create color gradients and apply all the watercolor techniques you've learned.

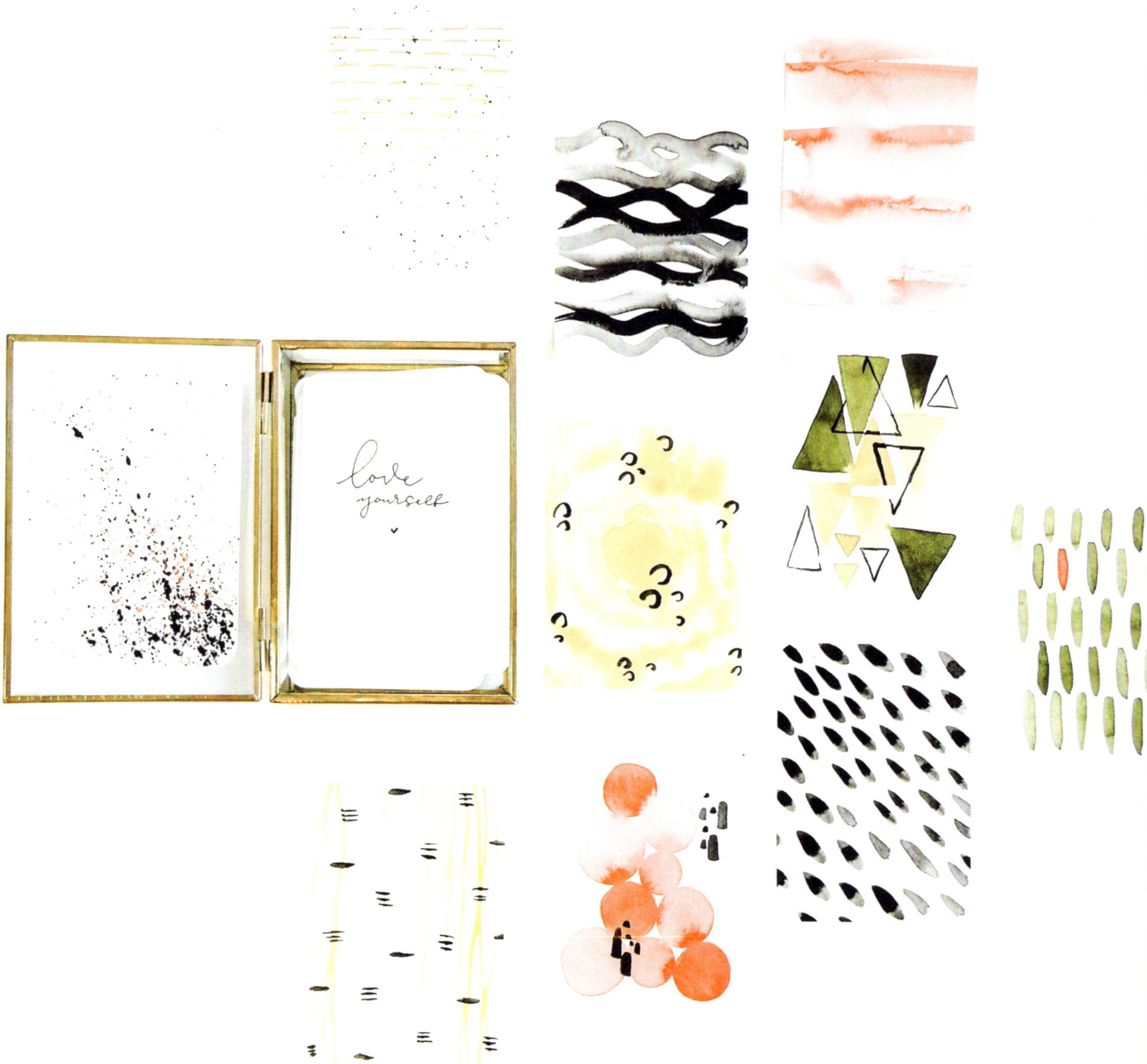

## MATERIALS

- Watercolor paper, postcard format
- Watercolor paint
- Watercolor brush
- Pigment liner

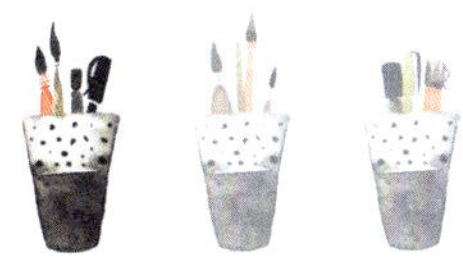

## Here's how to do it

1. Put together a color palette (you could even use the same palette you explored in the Abstract: Moodboard project) and start with shapes and brush strokes that you're already familiar with. Whether it's circles, straight or curved brush strokes, or even just speckles, make a start and set aside the first cards to dry.

2. When you've created enough cards in the first step, take the dried cards again and look to see where you can perhaps put more accents or details using a specific color. You can distribute them symmetrically over the whole card or just place them selectively and randomly. Not every card has to have accents – you can also keep some cards simply monochrome.

3. Now look at each card in turn and consider which saying or thought fits the design: see Inspirations: Sayings for some ideas. I've used a pigment liner for the lettering, but if you prefer to use a brush pen, choose one with a more robust brush tip.

4. Once you've finished creating all the cards and have lettered your sayings and thoughts on the back of each, look for a nice container to store them in, or display them where you can see them everyday to inspire and motivate you.

TIP: *If you package them prettily, you could give your inspiration card collection as a gift.*

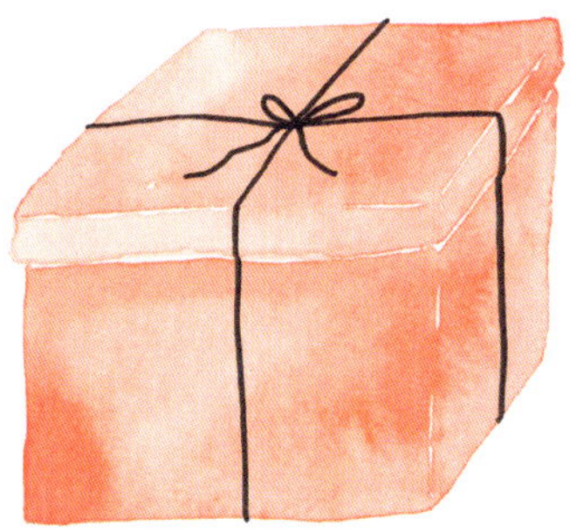

## Inspiration: Sayings

Use these letterings as a source of inspiration or a design template for your very own personal motivational cards.

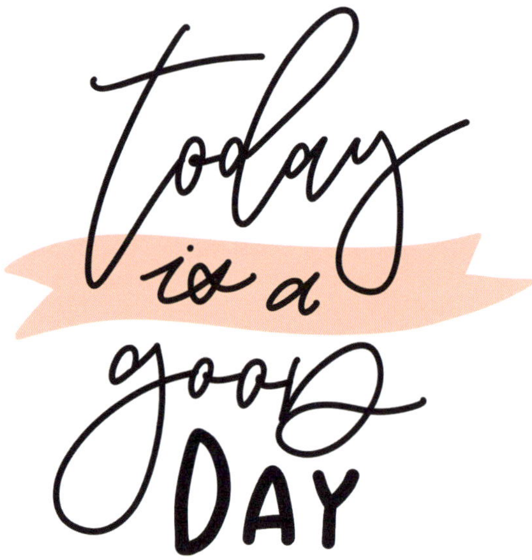


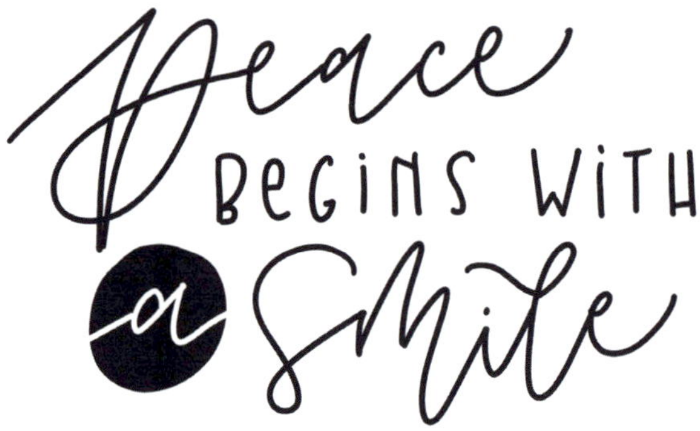


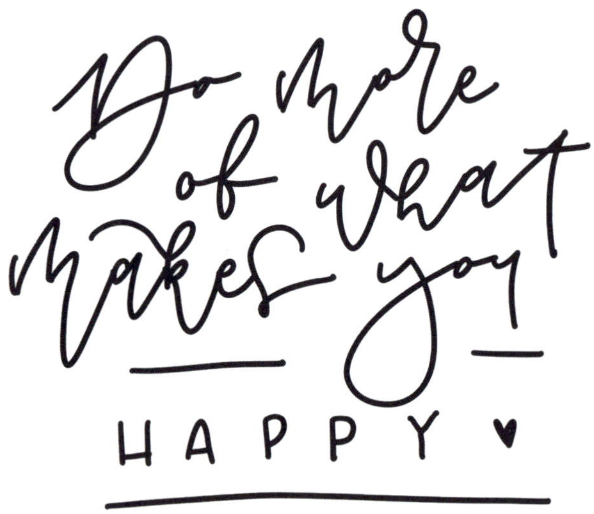


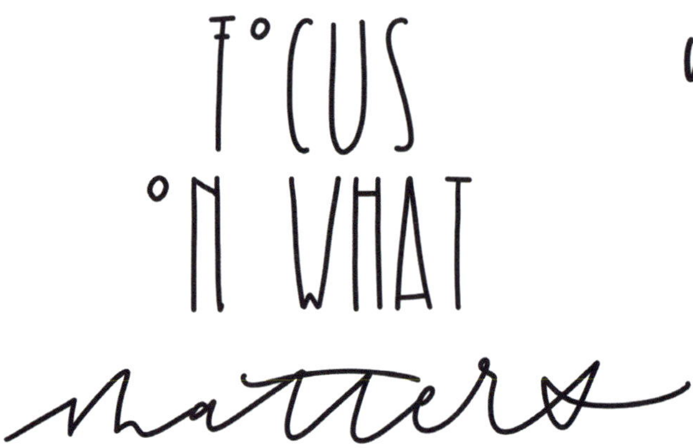

BE here NOW

peaceful mind grateful heart

YOUR ONLY limit IS YOUR mind

Don't stop until YOU ARE proud

kill them with kindness

TRUST THE TIMING of your life

# Seasonal gift boxes

Homemade gift packaging decorated with individual watercolor landscapes and scenes is a very special way to wrap gifts for your loved ones.

In this project, you can apply all the watercolor techniques you've learned in Basics: Watercolor Know-How. Take your inspiration from the seasons and think more abstractly rather than illustrating entire landscape pictures in detail. You can decide how simple or colorful you want to make the gift boxes.

## MATERIALS

- A variety of white cardboard boxes suitable for painting with watercolor
- Watercolor paint
- Watercolor brush
- Tissue paper (to wrap the gift box)
- Gift tags (black)
- Gift ribbon/cord
- Gel pen (white)

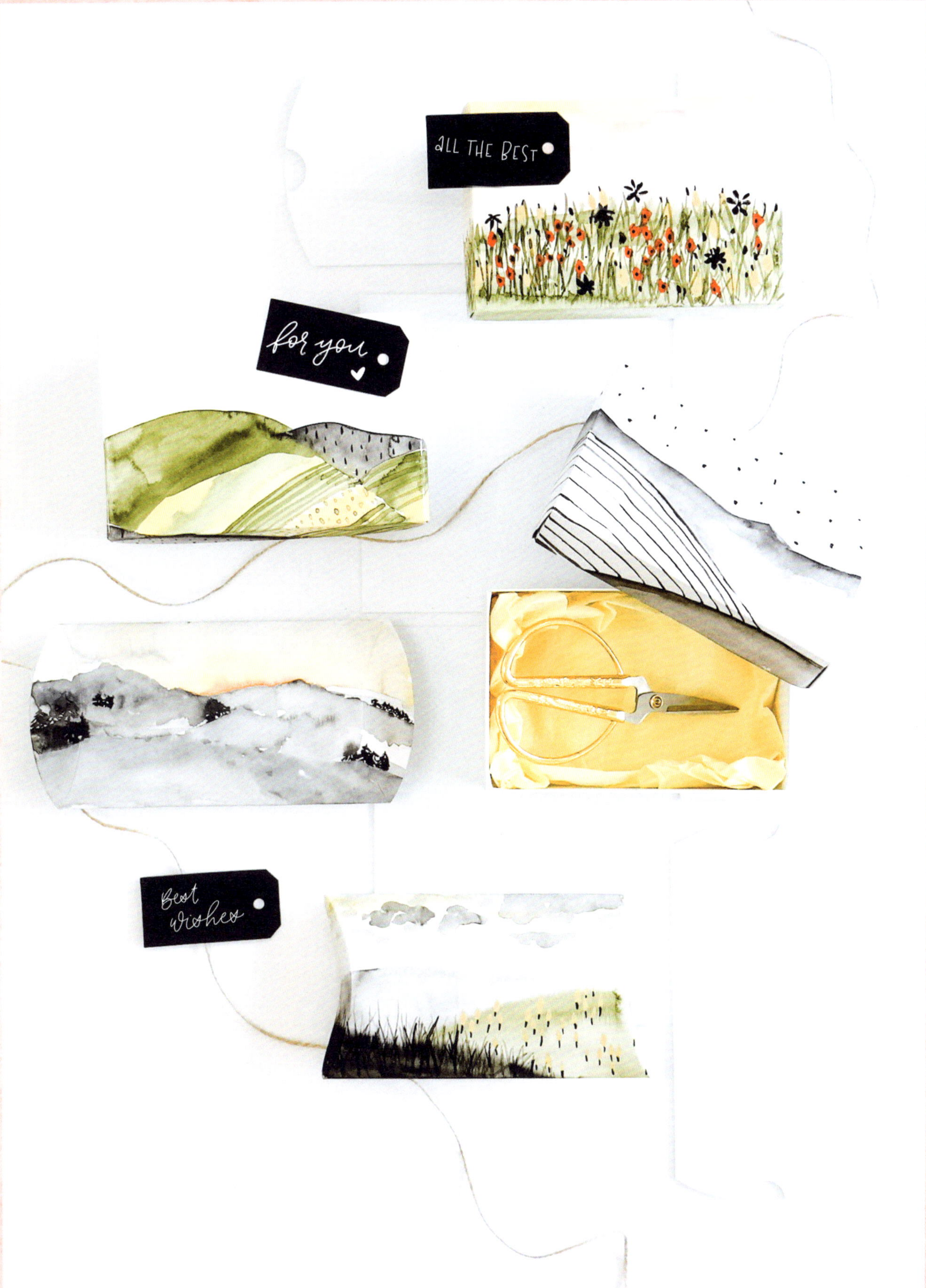
ALL THE BEST
for you
Best wishes

## Here's how to do it

1. Lay the cardboard boxes out flat and work on this project in layers. If you want to illustrate a sky, start by applying paint to the top edge of the lid and use the washing technique to draw it downwards by wetting the rest of the surface with clean water and connecting it to the paint surface applied above. You can control the color gradient somewhat by distributing it evenly with horizontal brush movements, i.e. from left to right and vice versa. For further watercolor effects, you can also dab clean water on the area or add more paint in certain places using the wet-on-wet technique. Allow this first layer to dry. If you want to keep the sky white, you can skip this step and move straight on to the landscape.

2. Try to form the landscape from light to dark. As you will see from the formation of the hills here, light areas appear more distant than darker or more strongly colored areas – these automatically move visually closer to the viewer. Add an initial, slightly more transparent, hill or landscape onto the gift box. If you want to delineate this area from the next one with a clear edge, leave this first landscape area to dry completely. However, if you want them to run into each other (as in my example), take the next step before the first area is totally dry.

3. Now you can paint an area, intended to appear visually in front, over the other area. In this step, use a little more paint to completely cover the first layer where these two areas now overlap. Repeat this step if, for example, you would like to illustrate a third hill in the foreground.

1

2

3

**4**. If the rear hill areas appear too transparent after drying, you can wet this area again and add more paint. In addition, you can also design the side panels and the top and bottom edges of the box in a different way. Alternatively, you can spread out the side panels completely from the start and illustrate the hilly landscape right across the sides.

**5**. Now add in details, including abstract patterns, grasses, tree silhouettes, snowflakes or even flowers, onto the individual landscape areas.

**6**. When your flat gift boxes are completely dried, fold them into their box shapes and wrap with tissue paper. Use a white gel pen to letter the black gift tags and, finally, use gift ribbon to tie the gift tag around the gift box.

TIP: *Instead of traditional cardboard boxes, you might also use pillow boxes for your homemade gift packaging.*

4

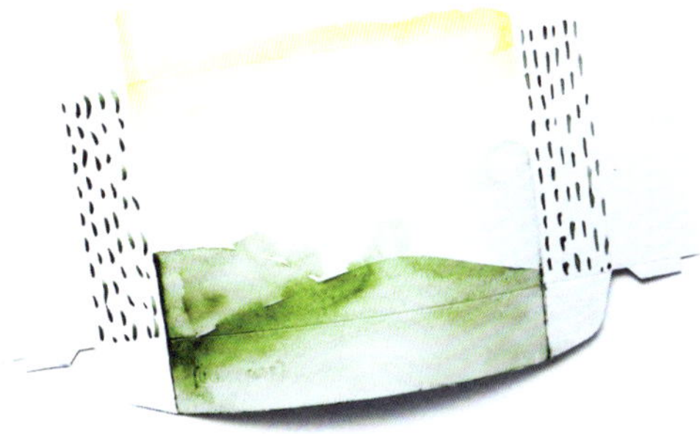

5

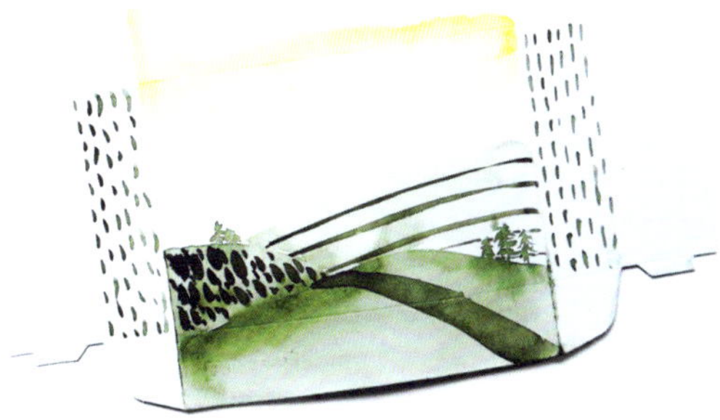

6

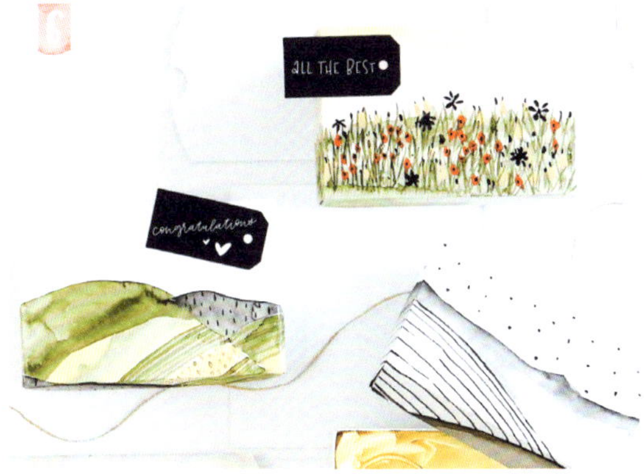


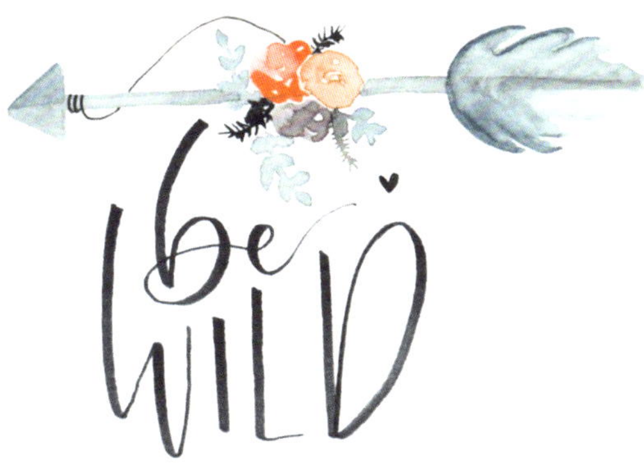

# Botanical table runner

Christmas comes but once a year – and lovingly designed decorations are absolute eye-catchers. Have you ever thought of creating an illustrated table runner for the Christmas table? This project is exciting to do because it goes beyond the usual paper limits by using a kraft paper roll.

Illustrating something on an oversized scale immerses you in new creative territory. Try not to make pencil sketches first, despite the larger size, but allow yourself to be creative with your spontaneity. Work your way along step-by-step and watch your botanical table runner gradually emerge.

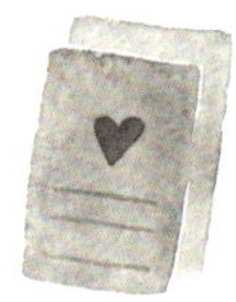

## MATERIALS

- Kraft paper roll (white)
- Watercolor paint
- Watercolor brush
- Place cards
- Pigment liner

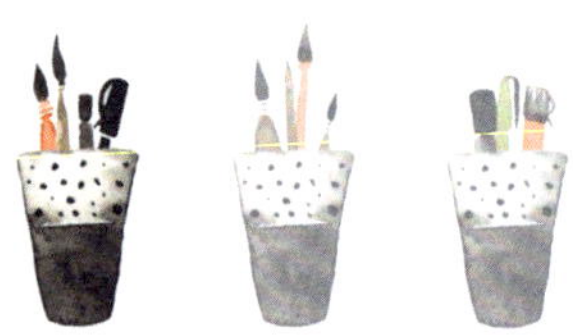

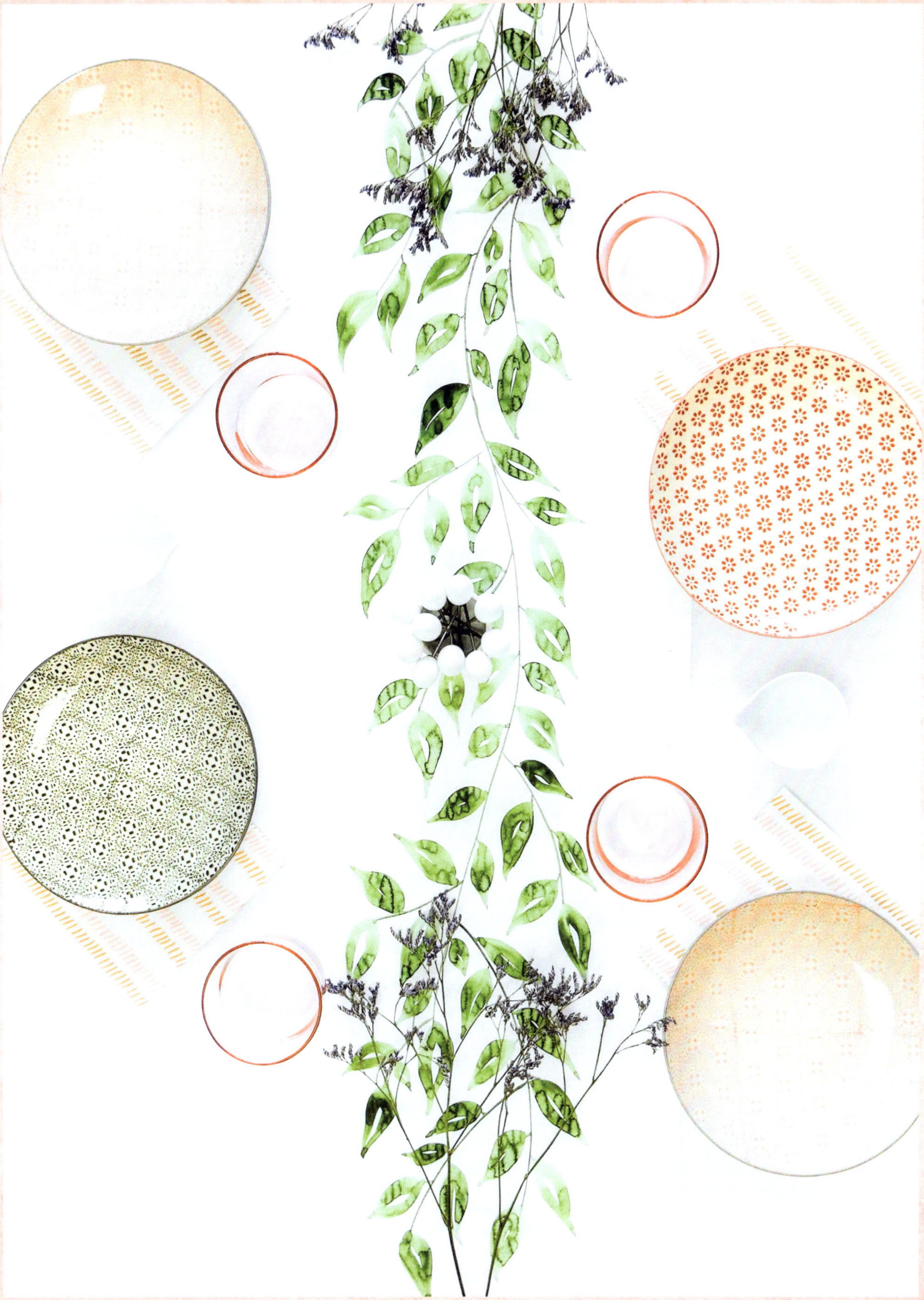

## Here's how to do it

1. Decide which leaf shapes you want to use for your table runner (see Inspiration: Leaf Shapes). Practice them step-by-step on a separate piece of paper. Do this by using the shape of the brush tip as an aid; place the brush on the paper, applying pressure and then releasing the pressure from the brush tip letting the leaf run out to a point.

2. Once you master the selected leaf shapes, spread out the roll of kraft paper, weigh down both ends so that it can't roll back up again, and begin to draw the first elongated stem with the brush and watercolor paint. In this step, construct a few branches too, so that the leaves grow in different directions.

3. Next, paint the leaves onto the pre-drawn stems. To give the entire botanical illustration more white space and separation, you can draw a short stroke directly out from the stem for each of the leaves and paint the leaf there, instead of putting it directly on the stem. Repeat until you're satisfied with the number of leaves and the size of the illustration across the entire runner.

4. Finally, use the pigment liner to letter the names of your guests onto the prepared place cards, placing one alongside each plate.

TIP: *Arrange a few real plants, leaves or flowers on the botanical illustration to give your homemade table decoration even more charm and style.*

4

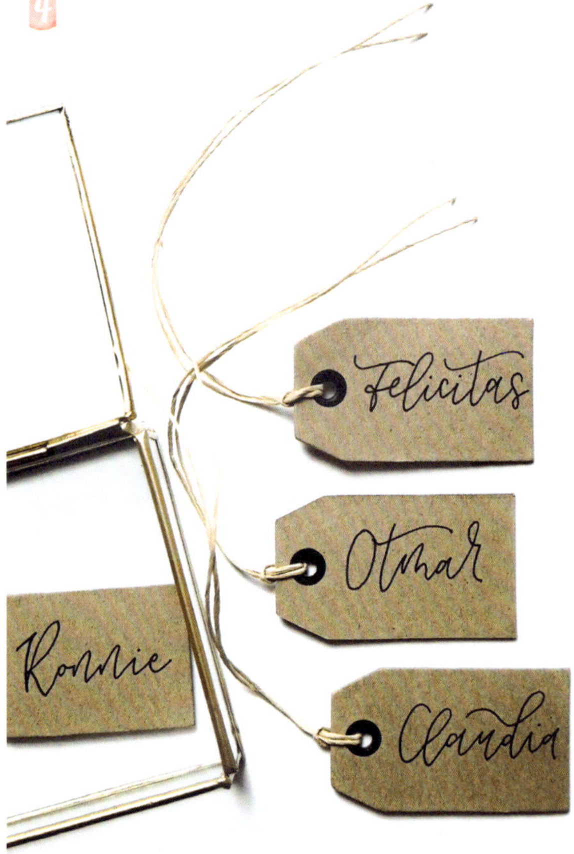


TIP: *You can adapt this table runner to suit the occasion; try choosing different leaves as a start point.*

## Inspiration: Leaf Shapes

I've put together some of my favorite types of leaf for you. Practice the different leaves step-by-step, then choose the ones that will transform your table runner.

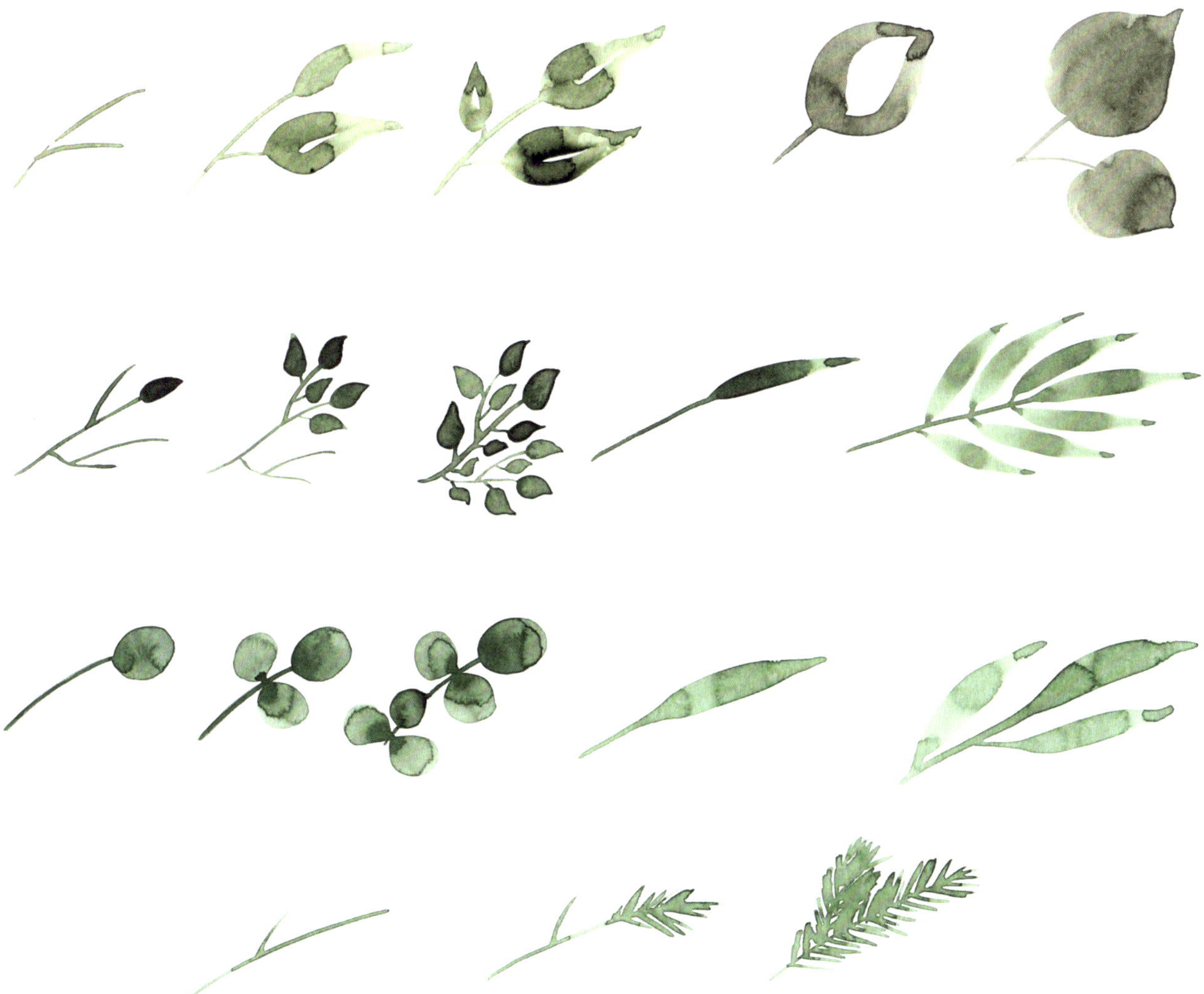

# Plant journal

The purpose of keeping an art journal is to work on a topic over a longer period of time, in order to see the progression of your development from the first to the last illustration. It will also help you to practice observing objects from everyday life with your own eyes.

You can use a single plant as a motif for your plant journal, or you can look to the incredible diversity of plants. Be inspired by your houseplants, or take photos of plants at a garden center. But try as far as possible not to use the work of other artists as a source of inspiration. Let your creativity and your illustrative understanding of plants run wild.

## MATERIALS

- Art or watercolor book (e.g. by Hahnemühle)
- Watercolor paint
- Watercolor brush
- Pigment liner
- Gel pen (white)

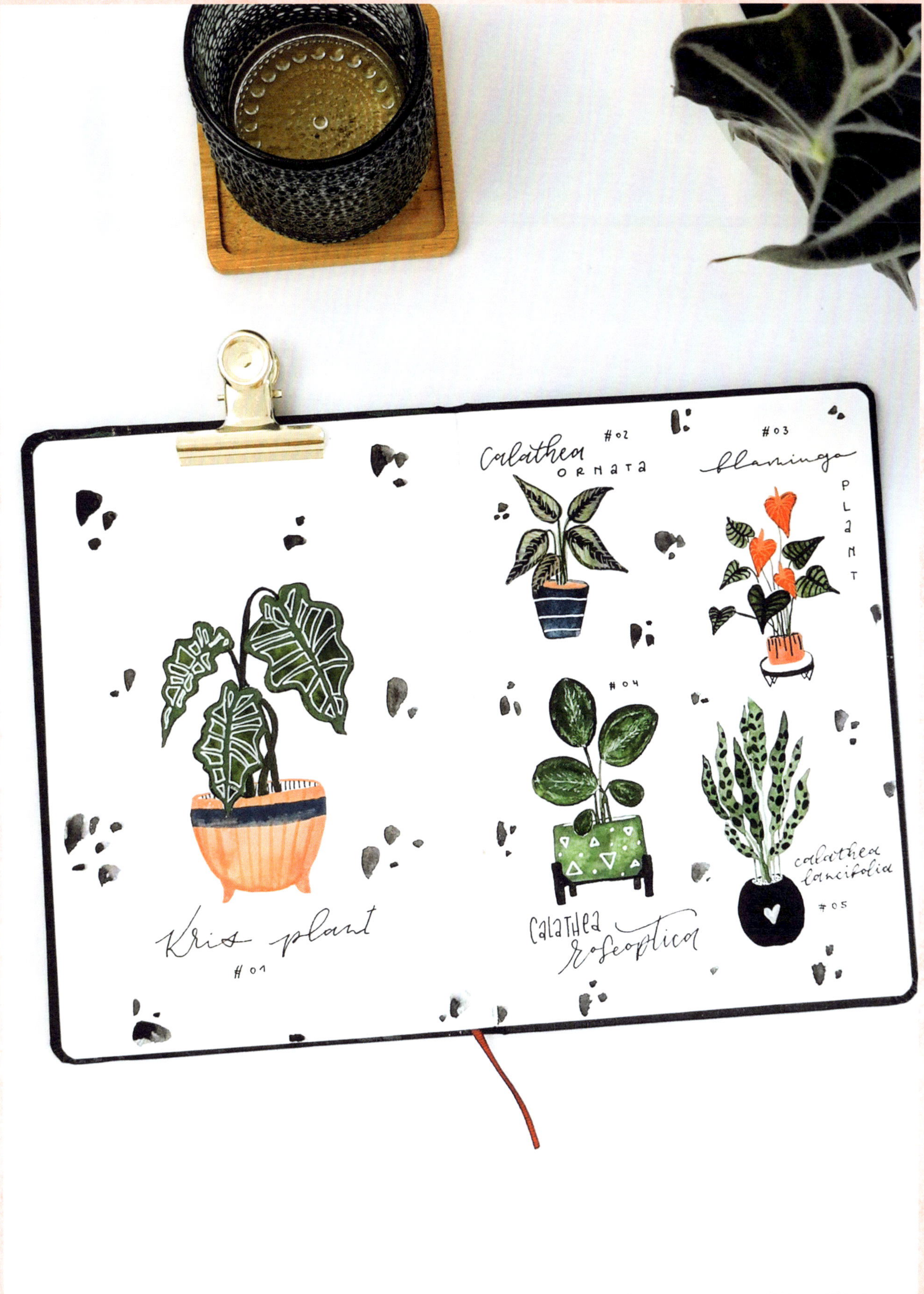

Kris plant
#01
Calathea ornata
#02
#03
flamingo plant
#04
Calathea roseoptica
calathea lancifolia
#05

## Here's how to do it

1. Before you make the first brush stroke, put together your color palette (either for the entire plant journal or for the one plant you want to illustrate). Make sure that you've at least two to three shades of green, both lighter and darker ones. The contrast between the shades of green is important, so that you can add the crucial plant details in step 5. In addition, choose a maximum of two to three different colors for plant pots and possible flowers.

2. Always start by illustrating the leaves. Take one of the selected shades of green and draw the contour of a leaf with the paintbrush. Take a close look at the shapes of the leaves of your plant. Try to keep working as quickly as possible and fill the leaf with the same color while the drawn outline is still wet. This way you can make sure that your leaves have as clean an edge as possible and that the pre-drawn outline is no longer visible. Paint all the other leaves in the same way. In this step, pay particular attention to the distances between the leaves. The more white space you leave in between, the more visible the stem becomes in step 3. If your plant also has flowers, paint them in the same way as your leaf arrangement.

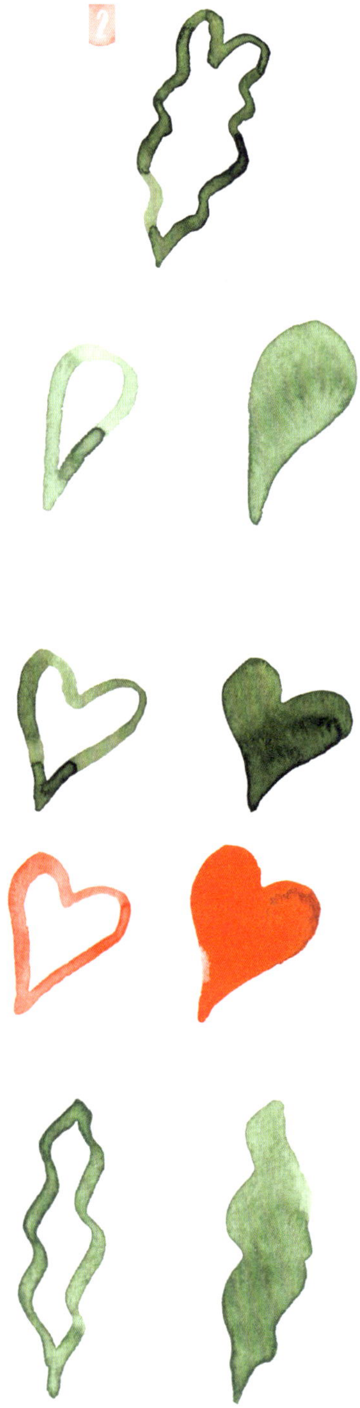

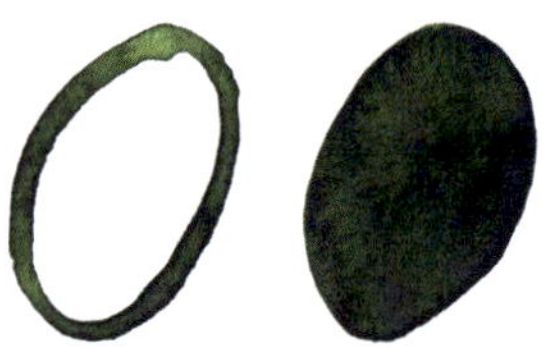

3. Once everything is dry, draw the stems with the brush more or less converging downwards. Finish the brush stroke for each stem approximately at the same height.

4. Leave the stems to dry and now think about the shape of the plant pot. Take a color from your color palette and paint an oval around the stems. This oval forms the top edge of the pot. Then you can finish drawing the pot shape with the brush and fill it in with the color used.

5. Finally, complete all the details – in my view, they embody the illustration of plants. In particular, copy the details of the leaves of your plant and think about how you can adapt them in a simplified way for your illustration. Do the same with any flowers. The plant pots can also be made more detailed by decorating them with a pattern, using your white gel pen also if you choose to. You may choose to place the pots on side tables or in another setting.

6. If you choose to, you can paint over the white gel pen detailing with water to soften the effect.

7. Use the pigment liner to hand letter the names of the plants that you have drawn.

TIP: *You don't have to just use contrasting watercolors for the plant details; you can also use gouache paint.*

6

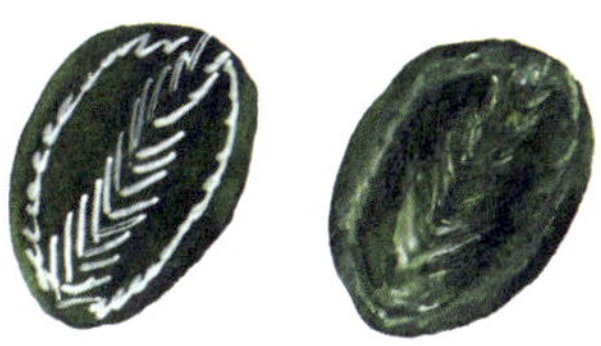

5

# Floral greeting

Make a loved-one happy by illustrating a vibrant floral greeting with gouache paint onto a black greeting card. You'll be amazed at the incredible color intensity of gouache.

Even though gouache paint is handled in a similar way to watercolor paint, the method of illustrating is a little different from the point of view of the design. Gradients and deliberately imprecise areas or contours are not the focus here. Instead, in my view, self-contained areas, clear contours and deliberately placed spaces are essential when it comes to gouache illustrated designs.

## MATERIALS

- Envelope (black)
- Greeting card (black)
- Gouache paint
- Watercolor brush
- Gel pen (white)

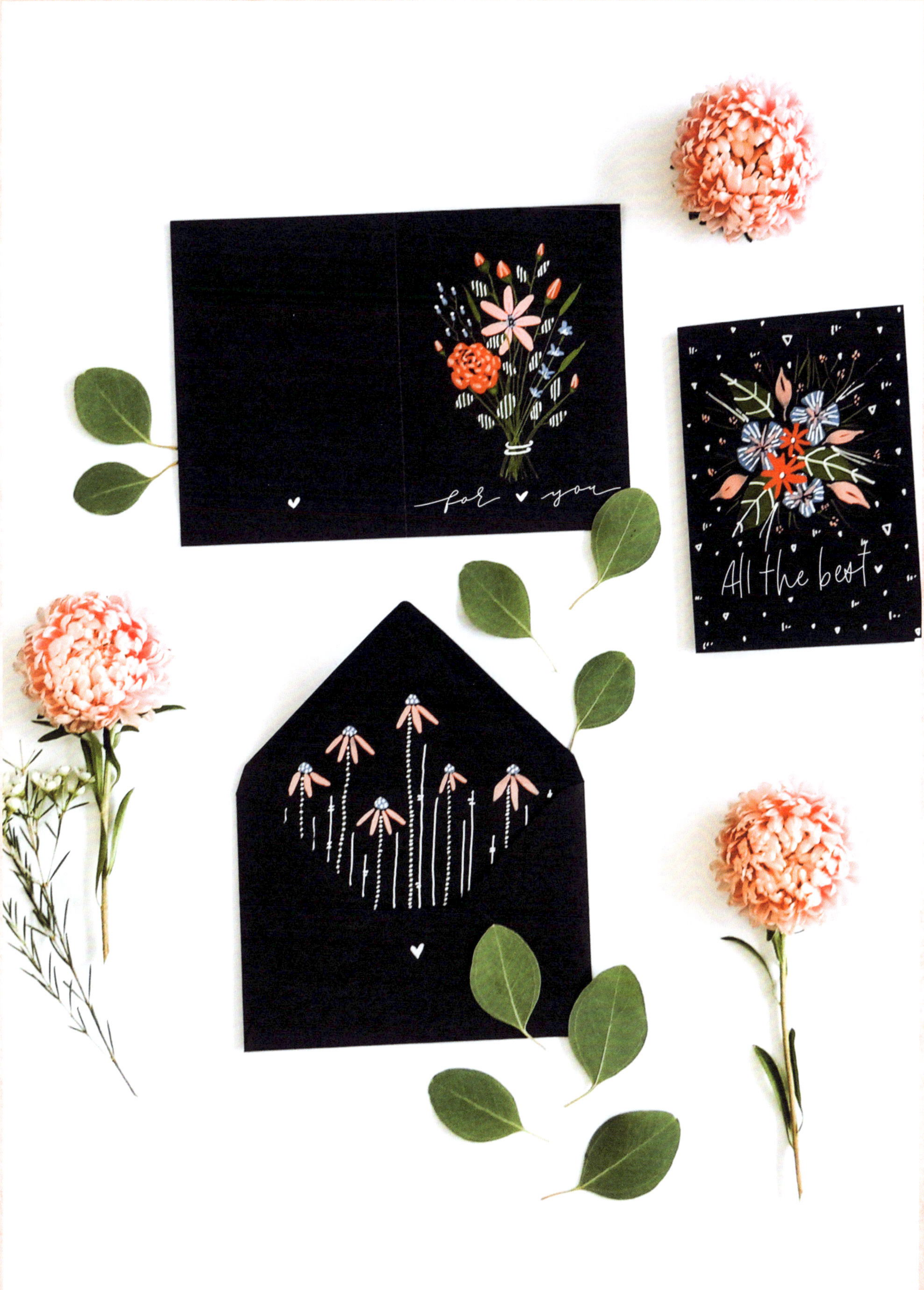
for you
All the best

## Here's how to do it

**1.** Start by putting together a gouache color palette with three to five colors for your floral greeting. Add a few drops of water to each color on your mixing palette, so that the gouache paint is creamy but not too liquid in consistency. The creamier the paint, the more opaque it is. The more you dilute it with water, the more transparent it becomes on the paper (as is also the case with watercolor paint).

**2.** Now practice painting motifs with your gouache color palette that you can use later in your floral greeting, preferably working on spare paper that is the color of your envelope and greeting card. In addition to classic leaves and various flowers, you can also consider objects such as grasses and buds, as well as abstract shapes and patterns to decorate your flower arrangement. Consider now whether you want to illustrate a bouquet, a loose floral arrangement or single flowers.

**3.** Select a few of the practiced objects and now move on to the envelope or the greeting card itself. Start with the largest flower and add a second larger flower some distance apart. Now add one or two medium-sized, as well as one or two smaller, floral elements to your design. Pay attention to a balanced distribution of the different colors. Then let the paint dry well.

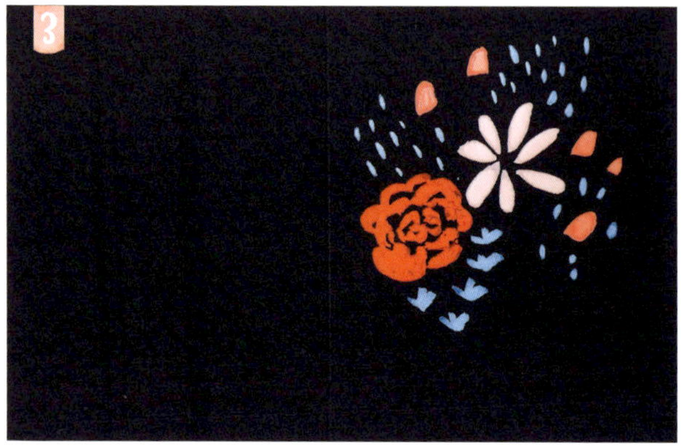


TIP: *If you don't have any gouache paint, you can also do this project on a lighter shade of paper with watercolor paint. Paint it a little more opaque and create your floral greeting that way.*

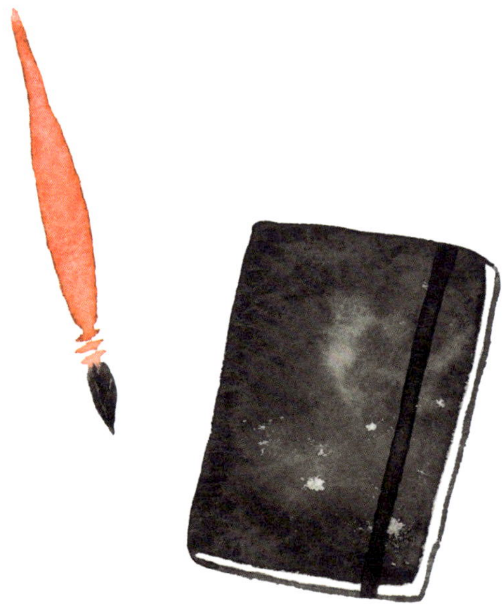

**4.** If you've chosen a bouquet as a motif, add a stem to each of the flowers and paint them converging downwards. To avoid accidentally smudging the paint, let the stems dry well. Then you can paint the leaves with gouache paint or with the white gel pen (see illustration for step 5), distributed over the entire bouquet, or just around your flower arrangement. Make sure that each element has enough space, and leave some space in between the items, so that they are still individually recognizable.

**5.** When you've finished arranging and painting the individual gouache objects into a floral arrangement and everything has dried thoroughly, you can start to add more details. Use gouache paint to add detail to the flower petals, or your white gel pen for finer details for the leaves or within the flowers themselves. You can fill in the background of the card with patterns also, if you choose to.

**6.** Finally, letter your floral greeting on the card using the white gel pen.

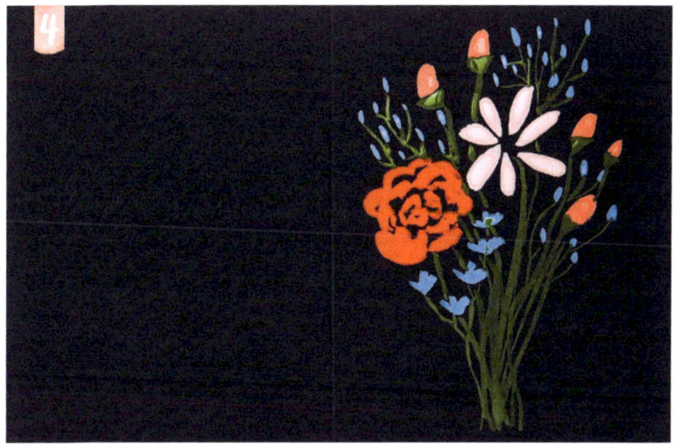


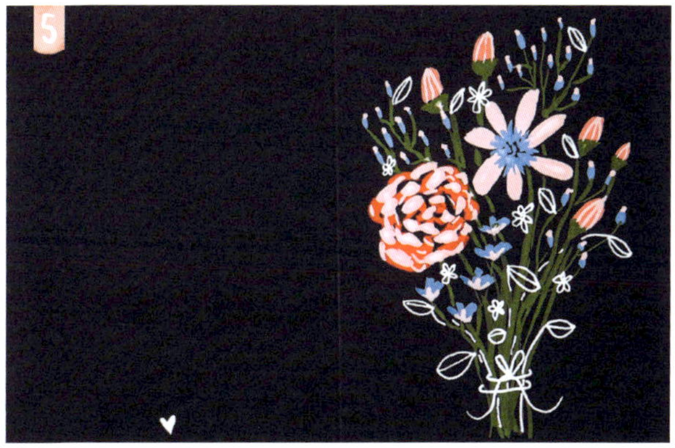


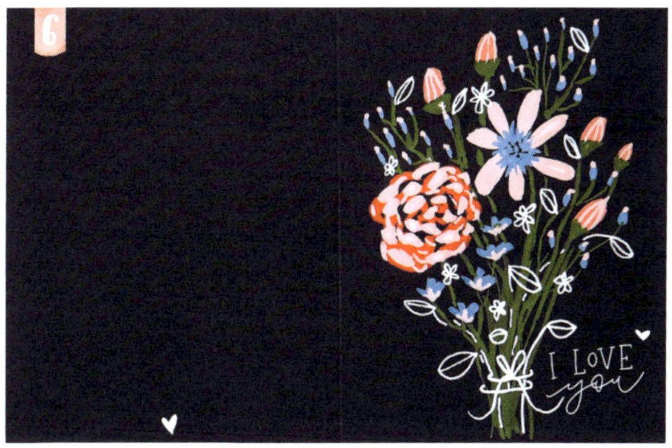

# Hoop art

For some time now, I've been fascinated by embroidery hoop art and its inspiring motifs. I wanted to combine watercolor and hand lettering with this fashionable hoop art movement.

After a few experiments in handicraft, I finally found a way to present my watercolor and hand lettering paper designs in an embroidery hoop. In this project, I'll show you step-by-step how to do this.

Get ready to be inspired by the world of hoop art, to decorate your walls with your chic creations or to give them as gifts.

## MATERIALS

- Embroidery hoop
- Mixed media or watercolor paper (max. 120lb/200gsm)
- Watercolor paint
- Watercolor brush
- Pigment liner
- Brush pen
- Gel pens
- Pencil
- Scissors
- Washi (or adhesive) tape

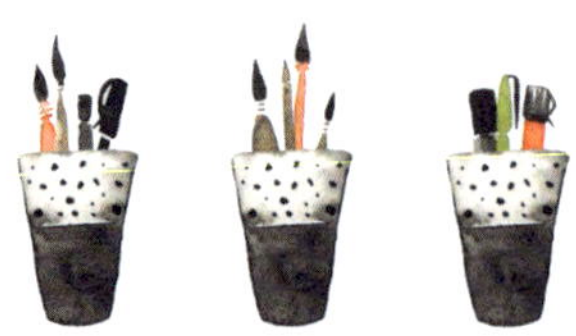

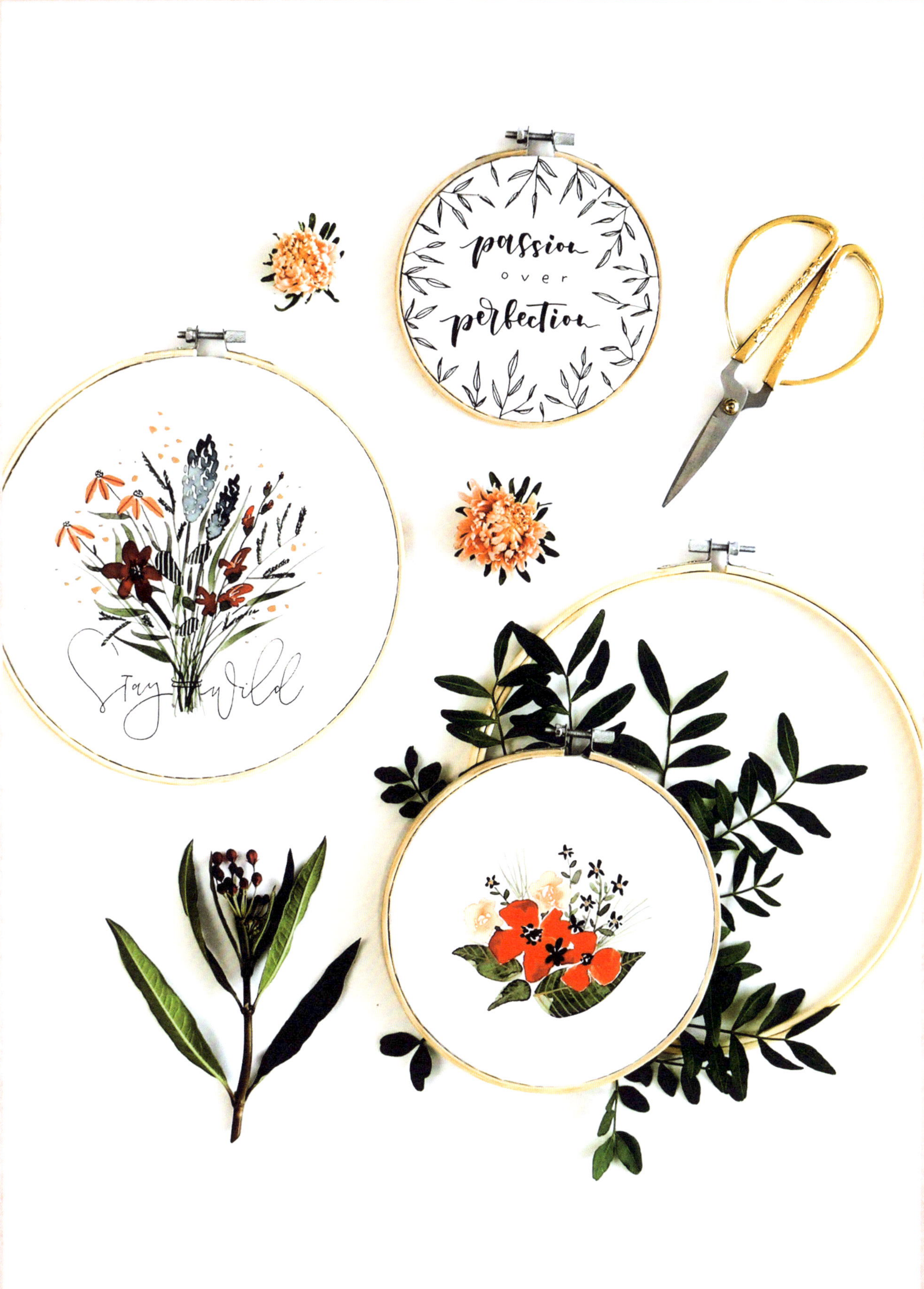
passion
over
perfection
Stay wild

## Here's how to do it

1. First mark the working area for your illustration. Take the inner circle of the embroidery hoop, place it on the paper and draw around the outside edge with a pencil. This penciled circle marks the area that will be visible once the paper is folded in the hoop later. Now start with the flowers. First dilute your desired shade of red with a little more water and paint the petals with it. While they're still wet, you can add another color accent to each petal with the original shade of red.

TIP: *Mixed media paper and watercolor paper are also available in larger sizes than you may have used for your work to date. So, if your embroidery hoop is bigger than your paper area, look for larger paper sizes.*

2. Once the flowers are completely dry, you can add leaves and other floral or botanical details to your arrangement.

3. Next add the stems of the flowers. Make sure that they are thicker at the bottom and become thinner towards the flower heads.

4. Now add the final details, such as the stamens (the dark dots in the center of the flower). Finally, add the lettering to your work.

TIP: *Even stand-alone lettering, without watercolor illustration, is enchanting in the embroidery hoop.*

1

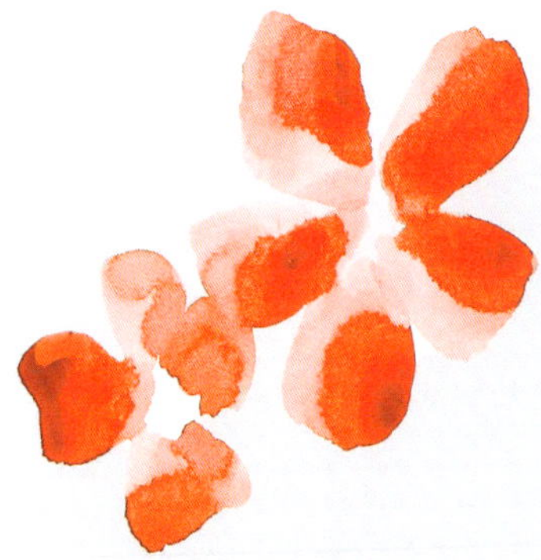

2

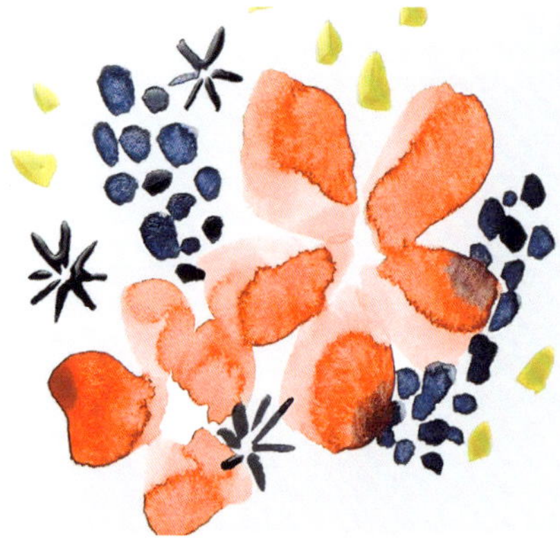

3

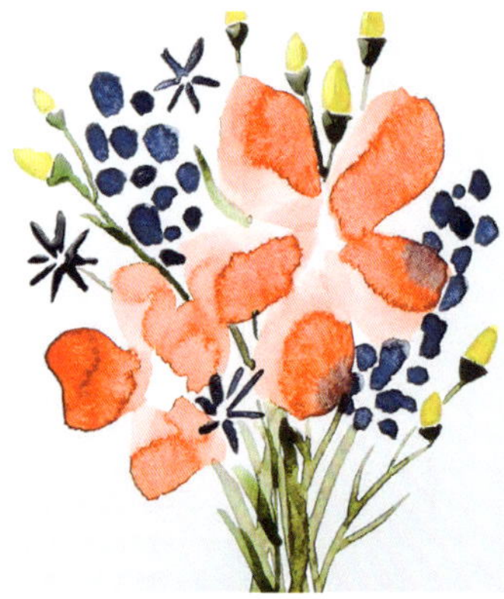

4

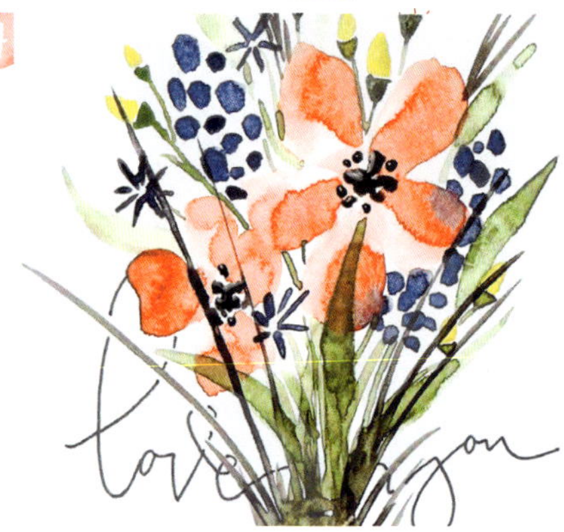

**5.** When your design is finished, take the scissors and cut out a circle leaving a gap of about 3/8–5/8in (1–1.5cm) outside the pencil line (free-hand cutting is completely acceptable here). Now prepare the paper for clamping. Mark an area of 3/4–1 1/8in (2–3cm) at the top of your work. Leaving this marked area uncut (it will be visible at the end due to the closure of your embroidery hoop), work your way around the circle, using your scissors to make a cut from the outer edge towards the penciled circle line approximately every 1/4in (5mm), stopping short a little clear of the pencil line, so that you don't see the cuts from the front on the finished piece.

**6.** Place the inner circle of the embroidery hoop on the back of your work within the uncut area. Then attach the paper circle to the inside of the hoop with two to three strips of washi (or adhesive) tape.

**7.** Now slide everything about a third over the edge of the table, so that you can gradually bend all of the paper cuts upwards, turning your work as you go. This bending will make the last step, the final clamping of the paper, easier for you.

**8.** To clamp the paper, turn the embroidery hoop over so that your work is on top. Carefully press the larger circle of the embroidery hoop over the paper so that the closure is at the top and screw it on tight.

TIP: *How about using black paper instead with a colorful design in gouache paint?*

5

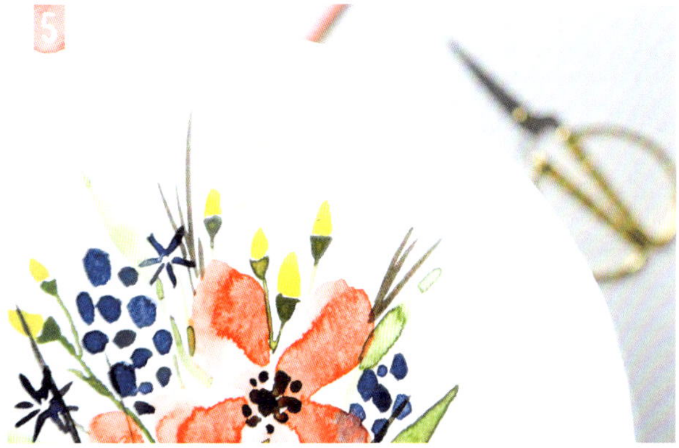

6

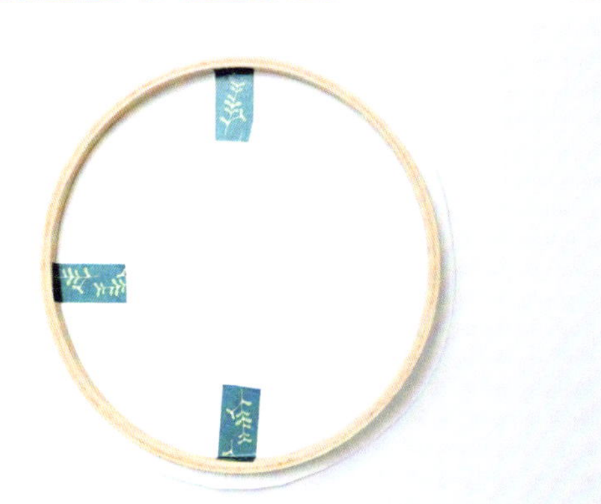

7

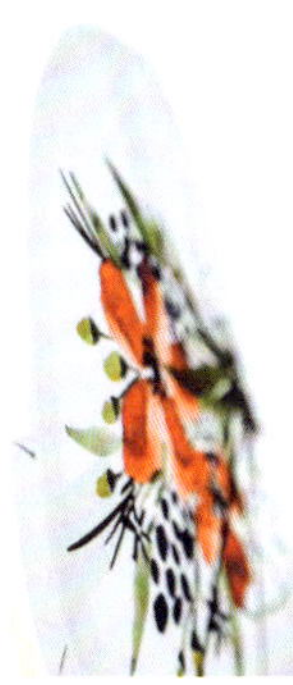

8

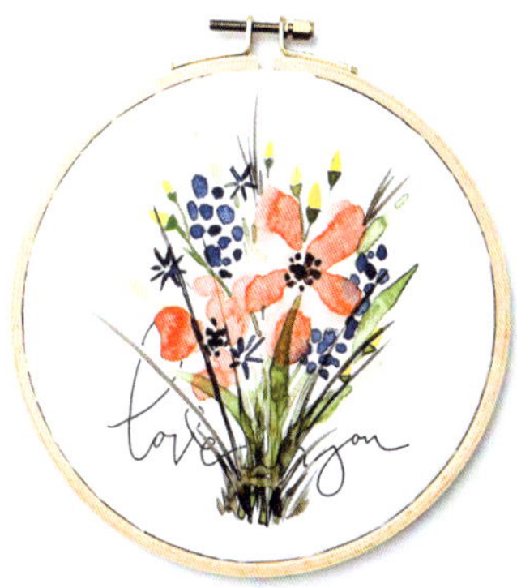

# Mounted 3D floral

Wreaths are beautiful decorations – whether real or in watercolor. Combine both in a 3D picture frame for a show-stopping decorative feature.

In this project, I'll show you how to create a watercolor wreath on paper without sketching in advance. Decorate your box frame with a few real flowers, blossoms and leaves, taking inspiration from their colors and shapes for your illustration. The result is one harmonious piece overall.

## MATERIALS

- 3D picture frame with mount
- Watercolor paper
- Watercolor brush
- Watercolor paint
- Pencil
- Cup or small plate
- Pigment liner
- Scissors
- Real flowers, blossoms, leaves
- Hot glue gun

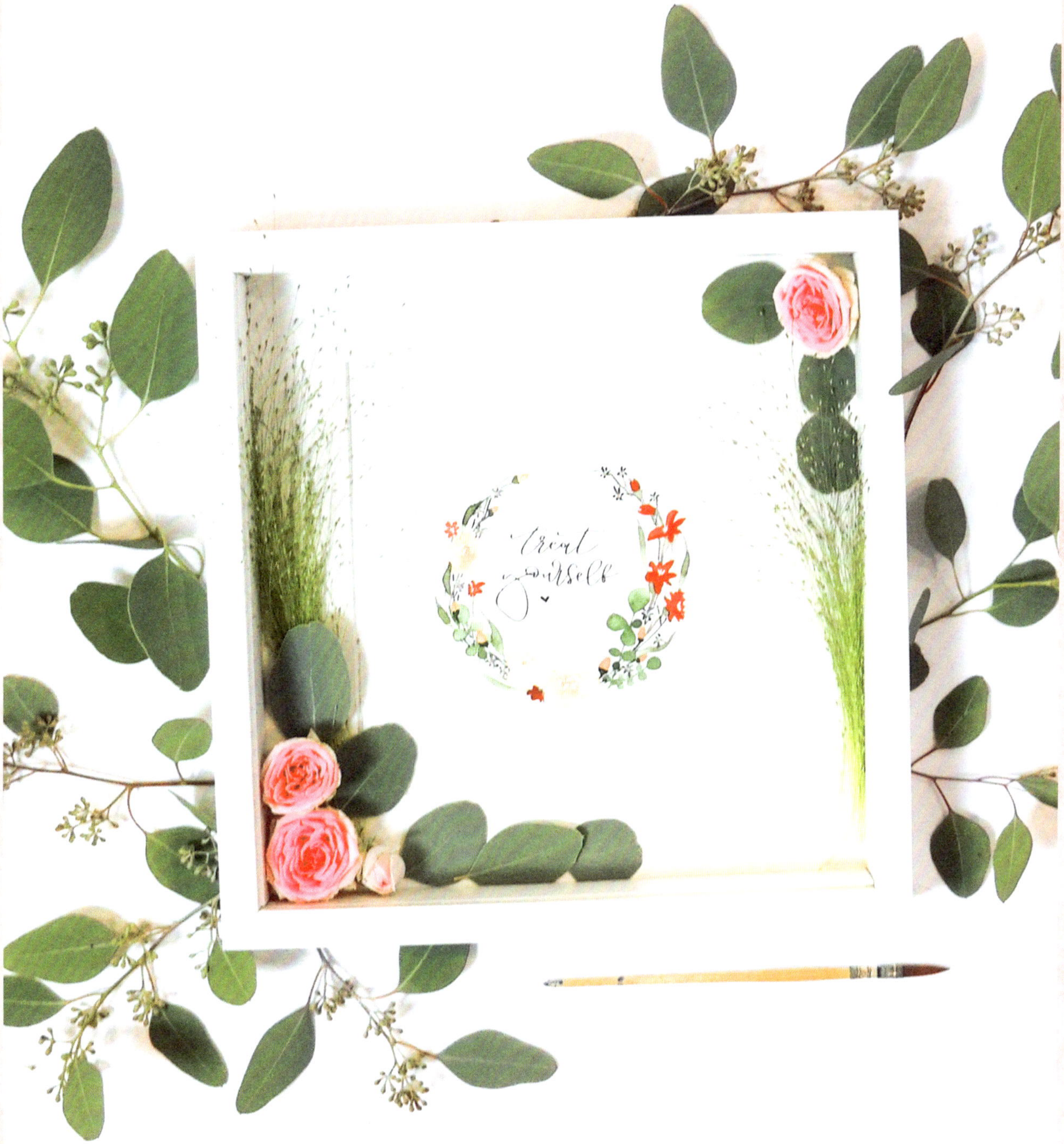
treat yourself

## Here's how to do it

Decide on the size of the wreath illustration to fit inside your 3D picture frame, then take a suitably sized cup or small plate and lightly trace around its edge onto the paper, using a barely visible pencil line. This pencil line is for guidance only and you should remember that you can't erase it once you've painted over it with watercolor paint.

**1.** Put together a color palette with a maximum of three to five shades to match your selected blossom and leaves. Start with the larger flowers and paint two to three of them directly on the pencil line. Add a few flower buds in the same color.

**2.** Now add one or two smaller types of blossom to your wreath in other colors. Make sure that you leave some white space inside the wreath to add the lettering later. Place the blossoms however you want, in fact you want to guard against your wreath looking too uniform.

**3.** Now add the final details, such as dark spots in the center of the blossom.

**4.** Paint the first leaves, then start connecting each flower and bud with a stem at the lower center. Once you've done this for each flower, you can compensate for any unevenness by adding a few leaves or other greenery.

TIP: *The direction of the leaves could all run in one direction, for example, clockwise.*

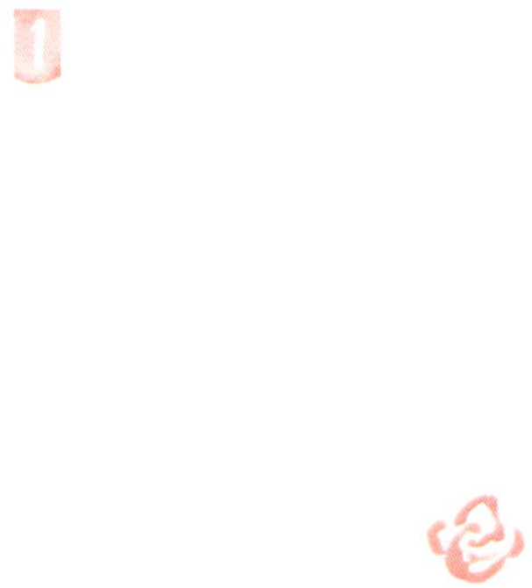

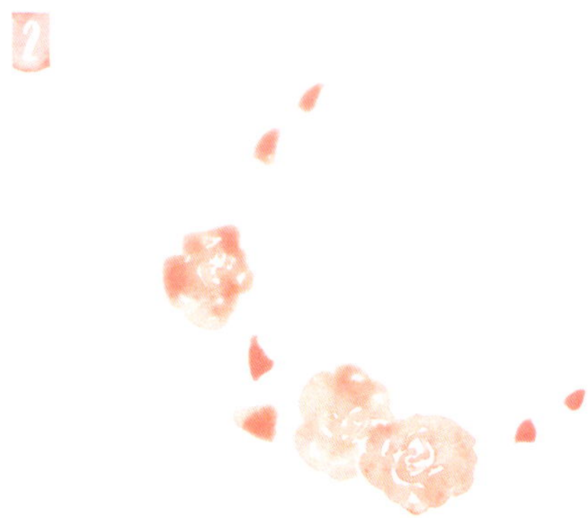

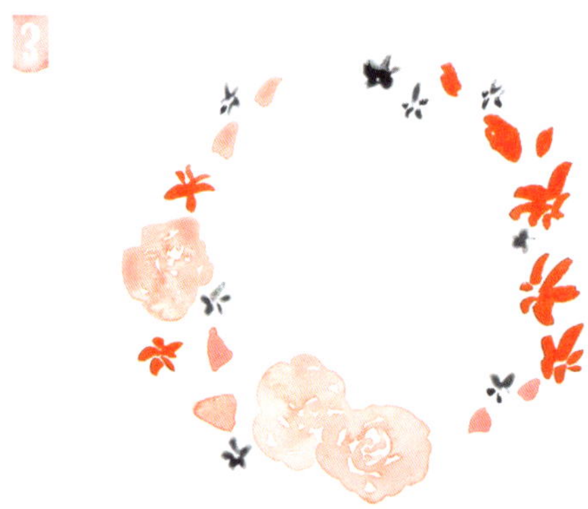

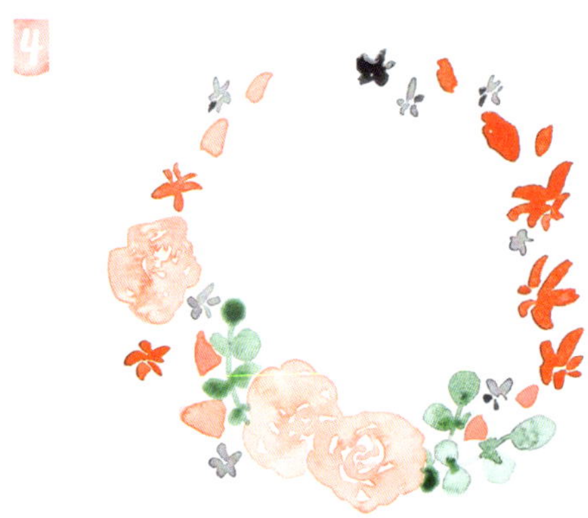

**TIP:** *As you add each of the botanical elements, let them dry slightly in between and only then start with a new type of blossom or leaf. In addition, when adding new objects, make sure that you leave a little white space distance from the motifs that are still wet. In this way, you avoid individual watercolor paints flowing too much into one another.*

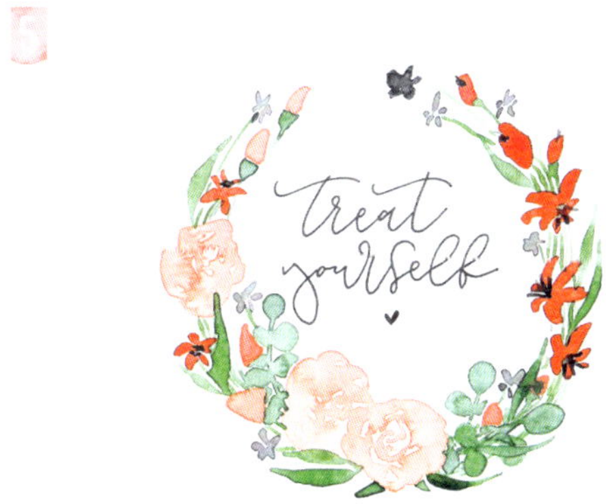


5. When everything is dry, you can add a few details to the blossom and leaves. In addition, you can now letter your selected saying in the wreath. Make sure that you leave some white space around the lettering and at the top of the watercolor wreath, so that your work doesn't appear overloaded as a whole.

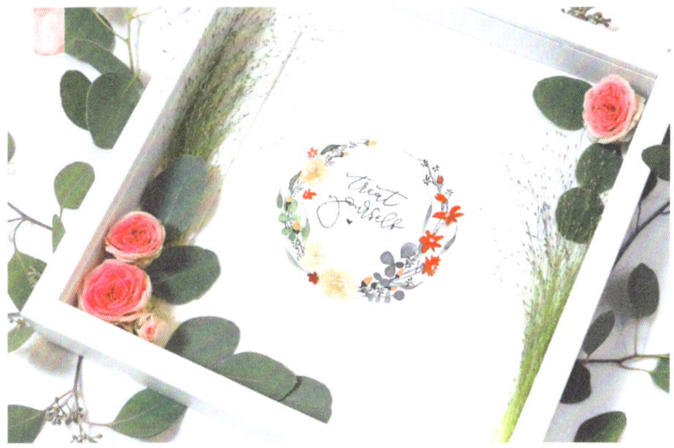

6. When your watercolor wreath is finished, take the 3D picture frame, cut the paper to size, place your work in the frame and fix the mount on top. Now start arranging your collection of real flowers and leaves inside the frame, making sure that you have allowed them to dry out a little before putting the glass into the frame.

**TIP:** *Attach the flowers and leaves directly to the mount, e.g. with a hot glue gun (alternatively, use double-sided tape or superglue). As long as you work on the mount, your original illustration will remain intact.*

**TIP:** *You can also use dried flowers and leaves. Remember to match your colour palette to the botanicals you choose to use.*

# Fruity labels

These illustrated and lettered self-adhesive labels are not only quick to make, but easy to fix on your jars.

You can create the labels with individual patterns and styles depending on the fruits you choose, and give them your personal touch. Who knows, you might even discover a look that will become the hallmark of your future work.

You could also scan, edit and print your artwork onto sheets of self-adhesive labels to produce them in quantity.

## MATERIALS

- Self-adhesive paper labels (optional: printer labels)
- Watercolor paint
- Watercolor brush
- Brush pen
- Pigment liner
- Gel pen
- Glass jars

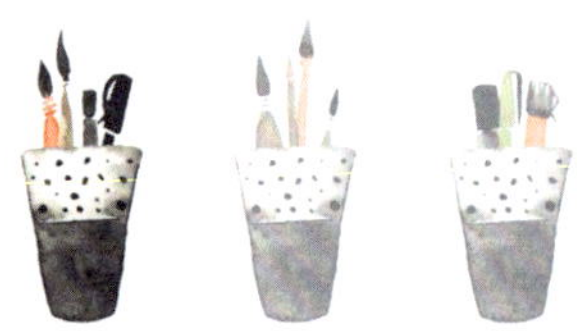

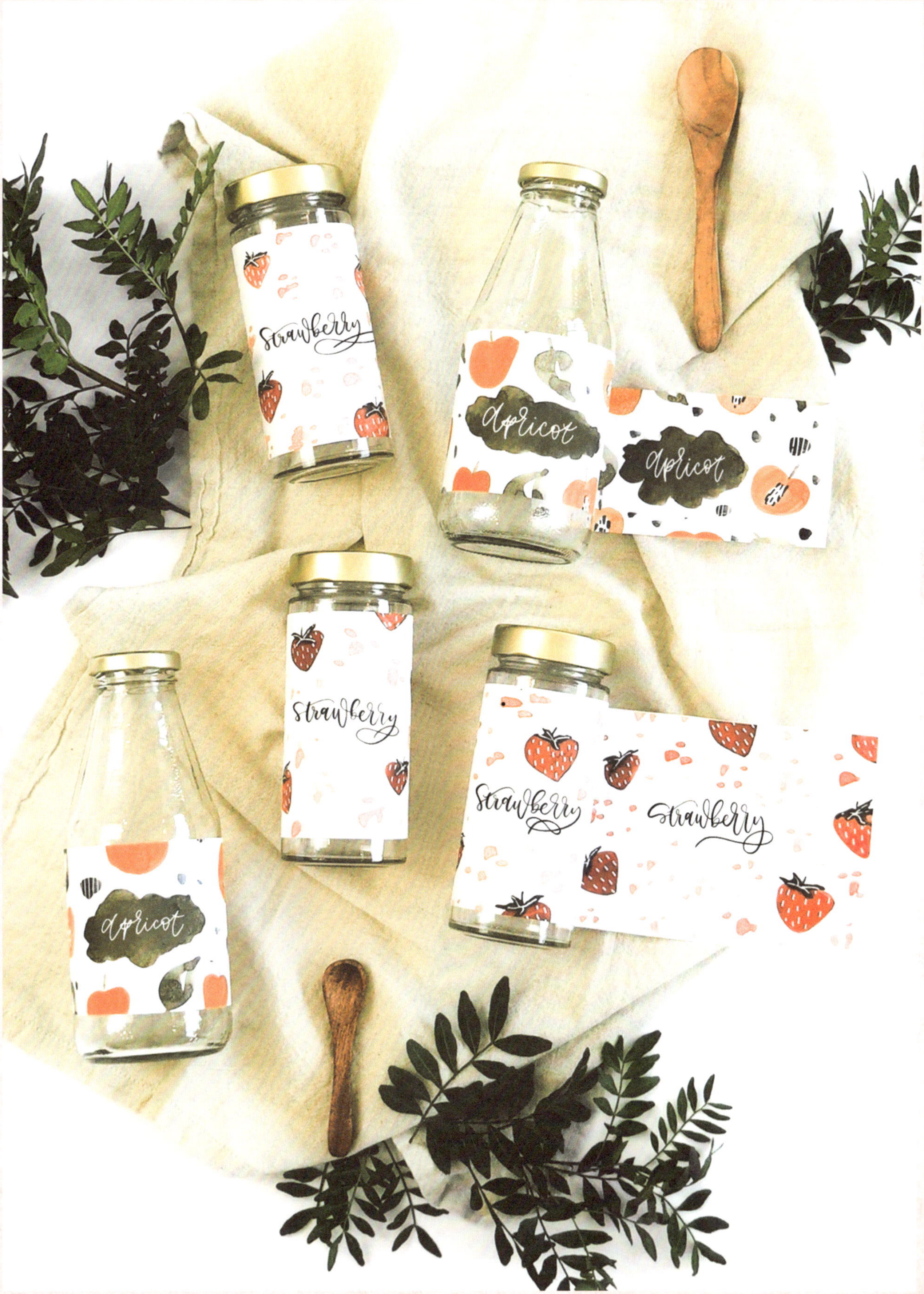

strawberry
apricot
apricot
strawberry
apricot
strawberry
strawberry

# Here's how to do it

**1.** Put together a color palette tailored to the fruit you have selected, and practice drawing this fruit on a sheet of paper. You can present it as a whole fruit, halved or cut into pieces.

**2.** Then take a sheet of the self-adhesive labels. Even though the surface of the labels is visibly smoother than that of watercolor paper, this isn't a problem. Don't work from label to label, but across the entire sheet, distributing the fruits randomly over the area. If you want to place the lettering in the center of each label, do bear this in mind as you work across the sheet.

TIP: *Place some of the fruits exactly on the join between the labels, too. Thus, when the label is detached and stuck on, it gives the impression that the pattern is continuous and the label is simply a cutout.*

**3.** When everything has dried thoroughly, letter the writing on the label. You can try out several different lettering styles using a range of different pens. You can also add other watercolor motifs in colors to match between the fruits and the lettering, such as leaves or abstract shapes, to visually fill the remaining white spaces.

**4.** Now you can detach the labels and stick them onto the glass jars. If the label is a little too large, cut it down evenly at the top and bottom, then stick it onto the glass.

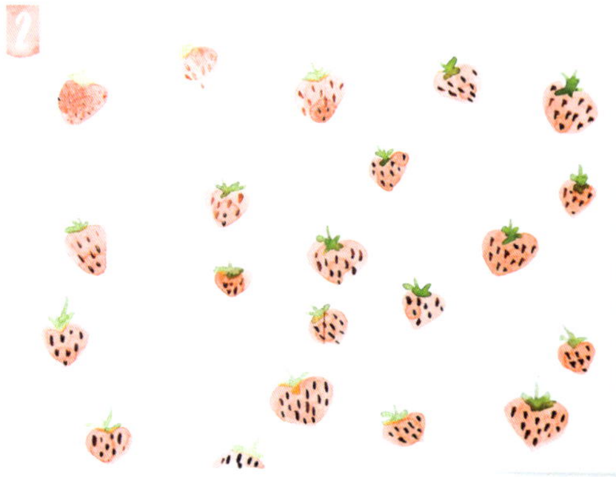


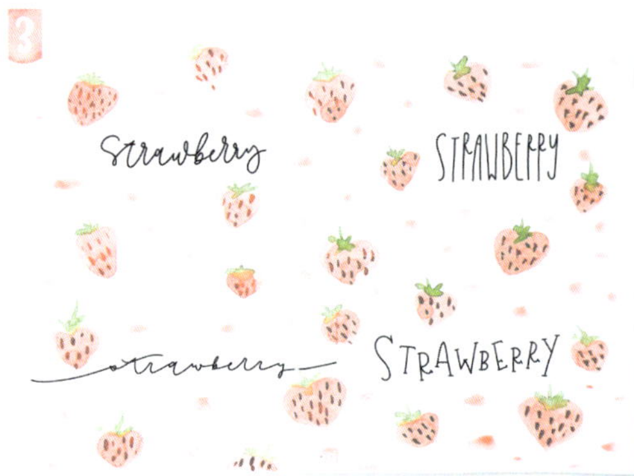


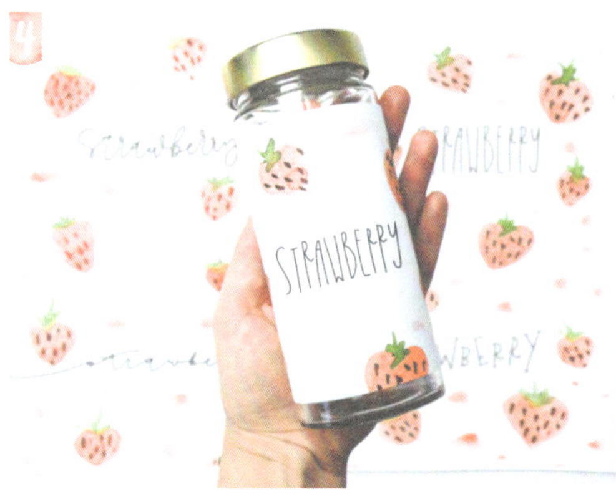

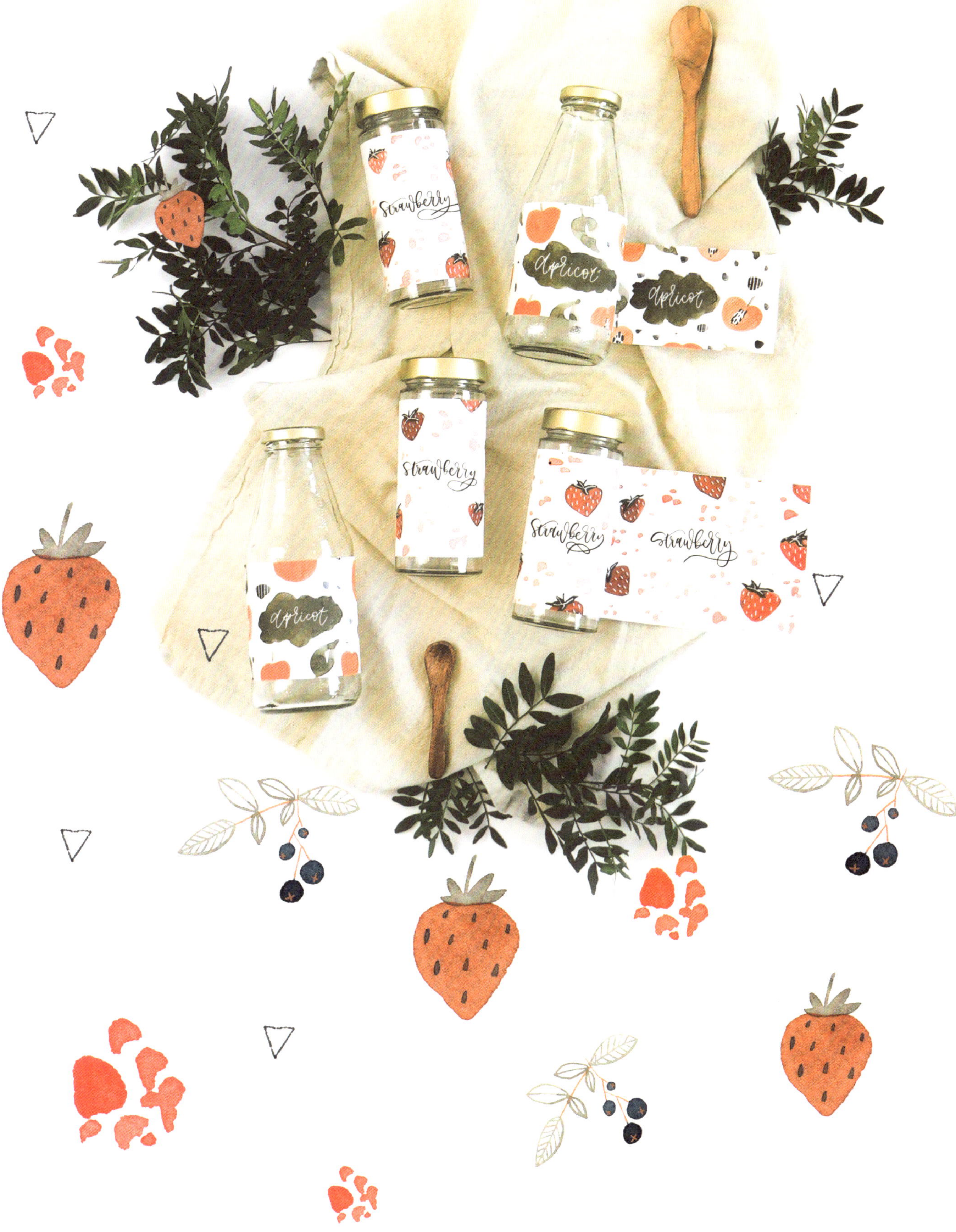
Strawberry
apricot
apricot
Strawberry
apricot
Strawberry
Strawberry

# Partyware

From the invitation to the welcome sign, the place cards to the menu – and the cocktail list, too – you can bring your own distinctive style to any celebration.

With this project, I'd like to show you how you can use a theme, in this case fruits, to give a coordinated look to a range of party stationery items. A consistent color palette, as well as the use of recurring motifs, will bring your partyware together.

If you prefer a simpler design than my colorful representation of exotic fruits, reduce your color palette to two or three colors and make fewer items.

## MATERIAL

- Watercolor paper (optional: watercolor paper, postcard format)
- Watercolor paint
- Watercolor brush
- Brush pen
- Pigment liner

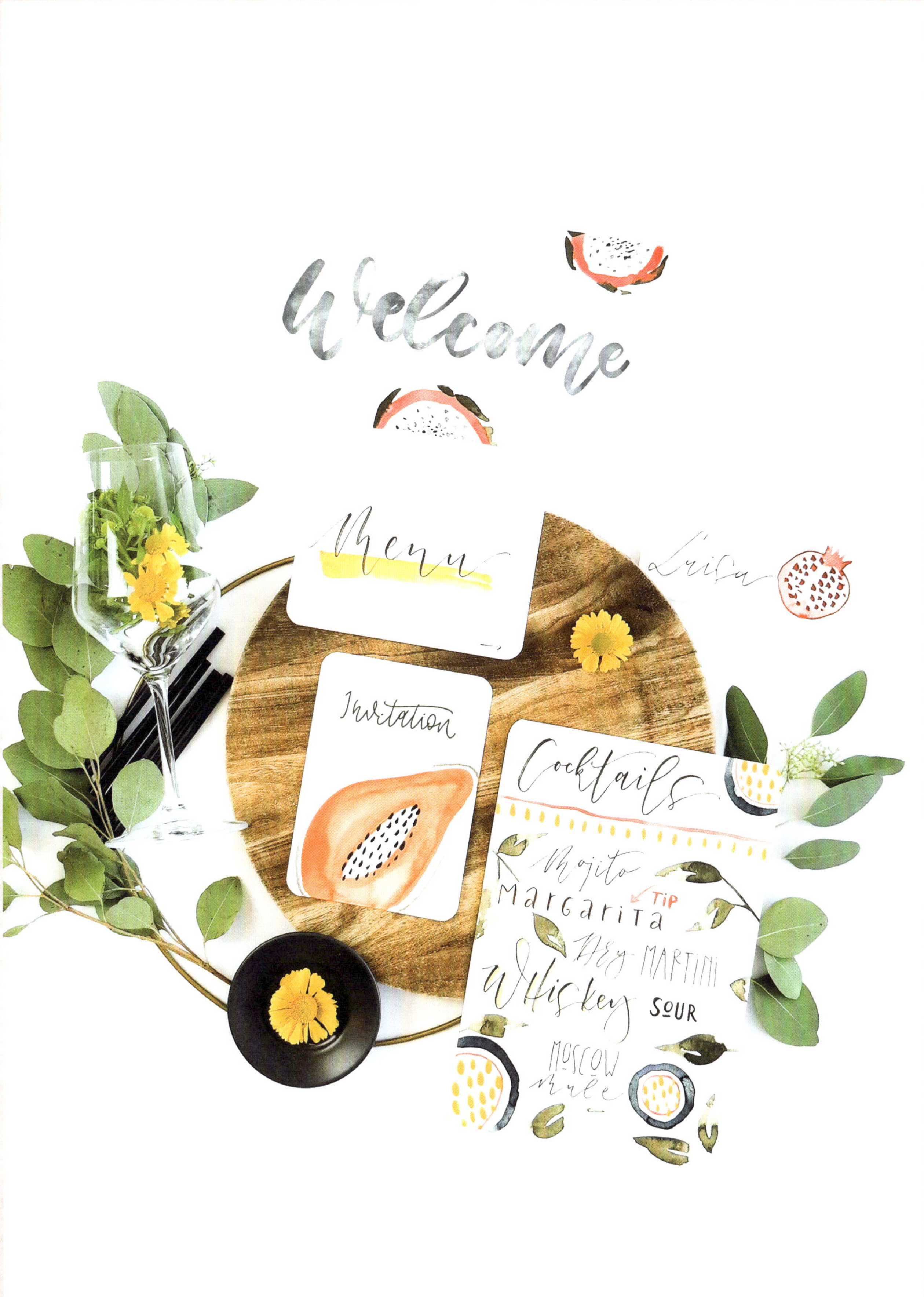
Welcome
Menu
Invitation
Cocktails
Mojito
Margarita
TIP
Dry Martini
Whiskey Sour
Moscow Mule

## Here's how to do it

1. Think about a general theme that will be reflected in all of your stationery items. Then, put together a suitable color palette and start by making a moodboard that contains all the illustrations and design elements that you would like to use for your stationery.

TIP: *To create the moodboard, choose a slightly larger paper format, e.g. A3, so that you'll be able to see all the motifs at a glance.*

2. Now decide what kind of stationery you want to use and how many partyware pieces there will be. You should also decide which motifs you want to use and which stationery items you want to present them on (I used papaya on the invitation, pomegranate on the place cards, passion fruit on the cocktail list, and pitaya on the "Welcome" banner). If you choose a simpler design, working with fewer motifs to create a more uniform collection, consider how you can roughly arrange your repeated motifs for each type of stationery.

3. Once you have an overall picture in your head for your partyware collection, start with the watercolor illustrations for each of the individual stationery pieces (but leave the cocktail list for now). My step illustration shows how I have painted the individual fruits step-by-step. Once your illustrations are complete, add the lettering.

4. For the cocktail list, it is best to start with the lettering, then add the watercolor motifs. Always work in a way that's easiest, according to the design requirements of your partyware items.

TIP: *You can letter not only with the brush pen, but also with your watercolor brush to achieve classic watercolor effects in your lettering (see the "Welcome" sign).*

3

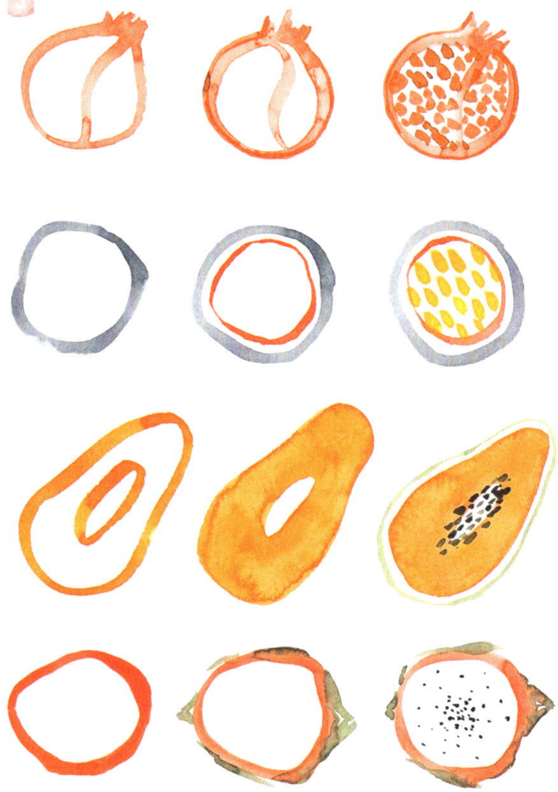

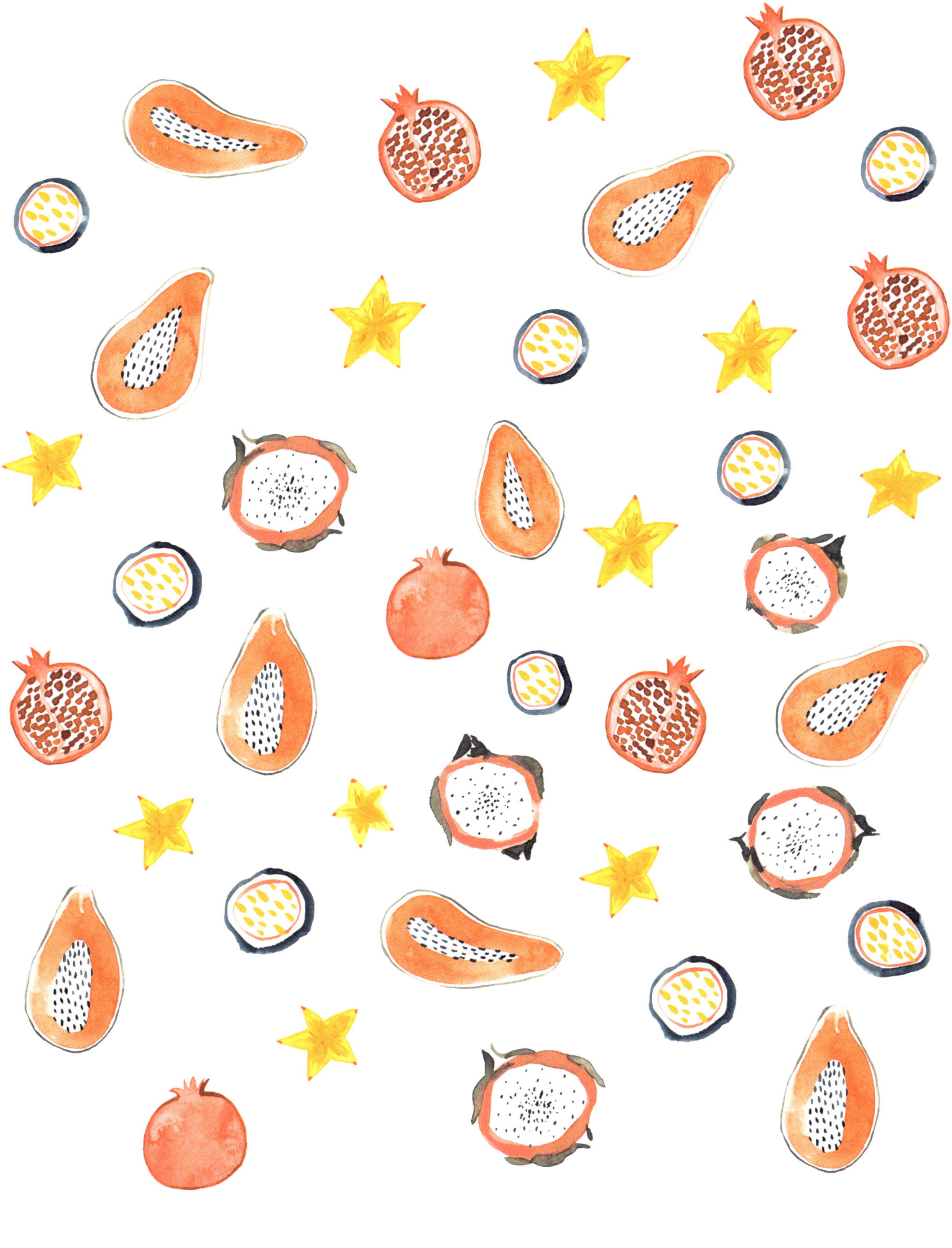

# Seasonal calendar

Create and hang your own seasonal calendar in poster format for an eye-catching decorative feature in the kitchen.

Use this project to delve deeper into the topic of fruits, explore and illustrate their diversity in your own way, and develop your hand lettering skills.

Rely on your creative flow and work your way through bit by bit rather than allocating specific areas to the motifs before you start. That way, you can concentrate on the painting process for each individual fruit and decide one-by-one how much space you want to allow.

## MATERIALS

- Watercolor paper (larger paper format, e.g. A3)
- Watercolor paint
- Watercolor brush
- Pigment liner
- Gel pen

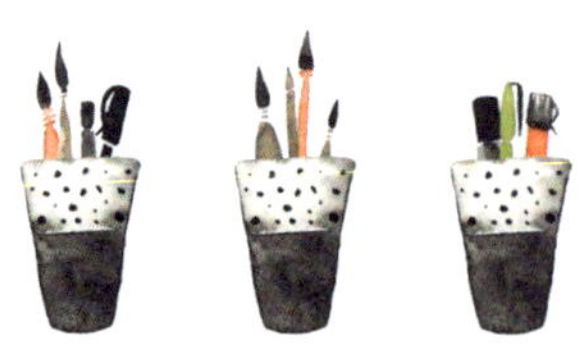

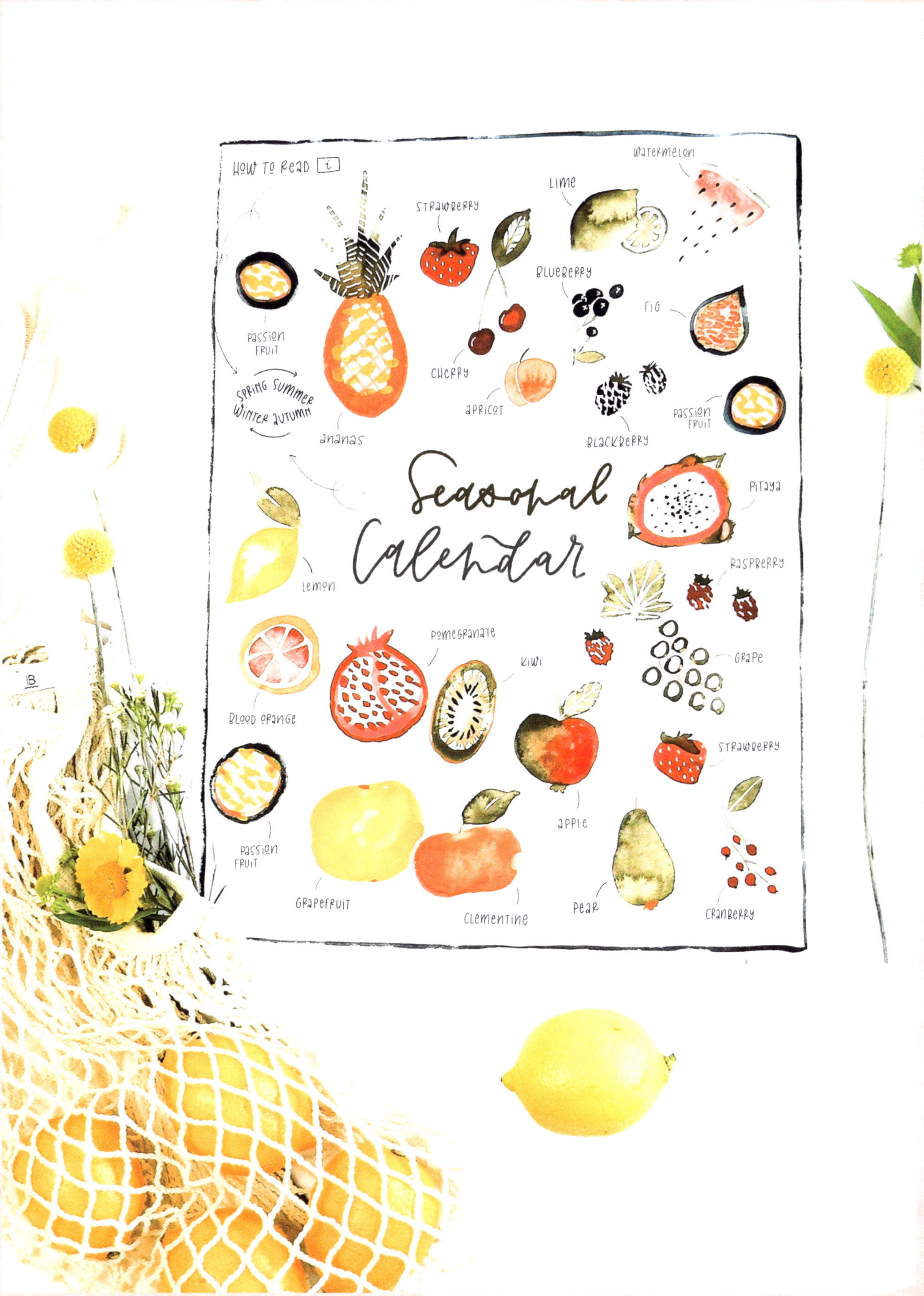
How to read i
Passion fruit
Spring Summer Winter Autumn
ananas
Strawberry
Cherry
apricot
Lime
Blueberry
Watermelon
Fig
Blackberry
Passion fruit
Seasonal Calendar
Pitaya
Lemon
Raspberry
Pomegranate
Kiwi
Grape
Blood orange
Strawberry
apple
Passion fruit
Grapefruit
Clementine
Pear
Cranberry

## Here's how to do it

1. Start with the lettering for the words "Seasonal calendar" (on one or two lines depending on the lettering style). You can do this lettering with a brush and watercolor paint, or, alternatively, use a brush pen of your choice. Position the lettering approximately in the middle of the paper.

2. Now write down on another piece of paper all the fruits that you want to integrate into your seasonal calendar. I've designed mine in such a way that you can "read" it clockwise from the top left: spring, summer, fall, winter.

TIP: *Categorize your selected fruits in advance according to the seasons – that way, you'll develop a feeling for how many fruits you need and roughly where they should be placed on your poster.*

3. Now, with the selected fruits in the back of your mind, put together your individual color palette and make a few illustrations on another piece of paper before you start illustrating directly onto your seasonal calendar. Remember little elements such as, for example, abstract patterns that you've used in other projects, and consider if you could integrate these into your fruit designs. In this way, your work begins to be more recognizable, and you can continue to refine your own style and method of representation.

TIP: *When illustrating the seasonal fruits, think more in a two-dimensional rather than three-dimensional way. The more pared back and abstract the presentation of your selected fruits, the more freedom you have to interpret them in your own way.*

4

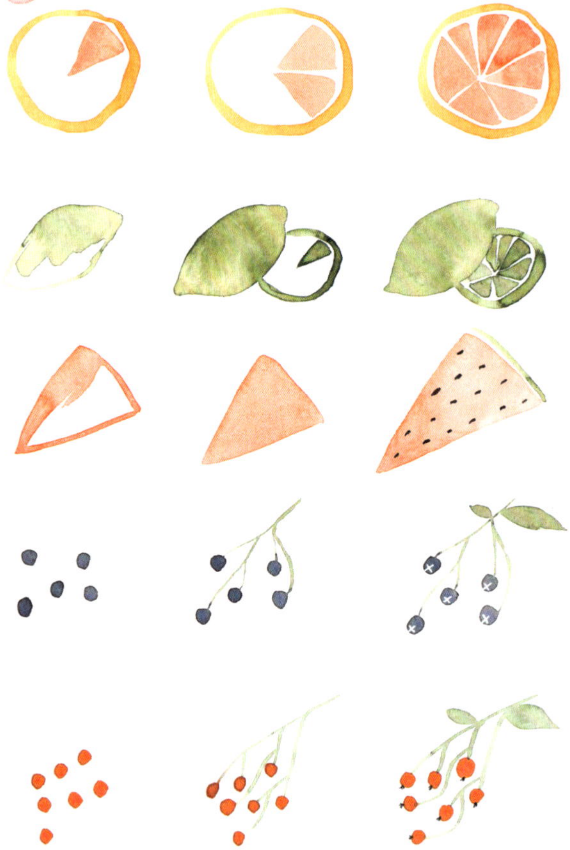

4. Illustrate the first fruits on your poster where possible in freehand. When one fruit is finished, start on the next one. Some of the fruits can appear on your poster several times, if they thrive all year round. My step illustration shows how I have painted the individual fruits step-by-step, and you'll find more in the Partyware chapter.

5. Finally, you can add descriptive lettering to all the fruits and paint a frame in watercolor all around to give your work a border that visually holds all your fruits together.

TIP: *How about painting a vegetable seasonal calendar next?*

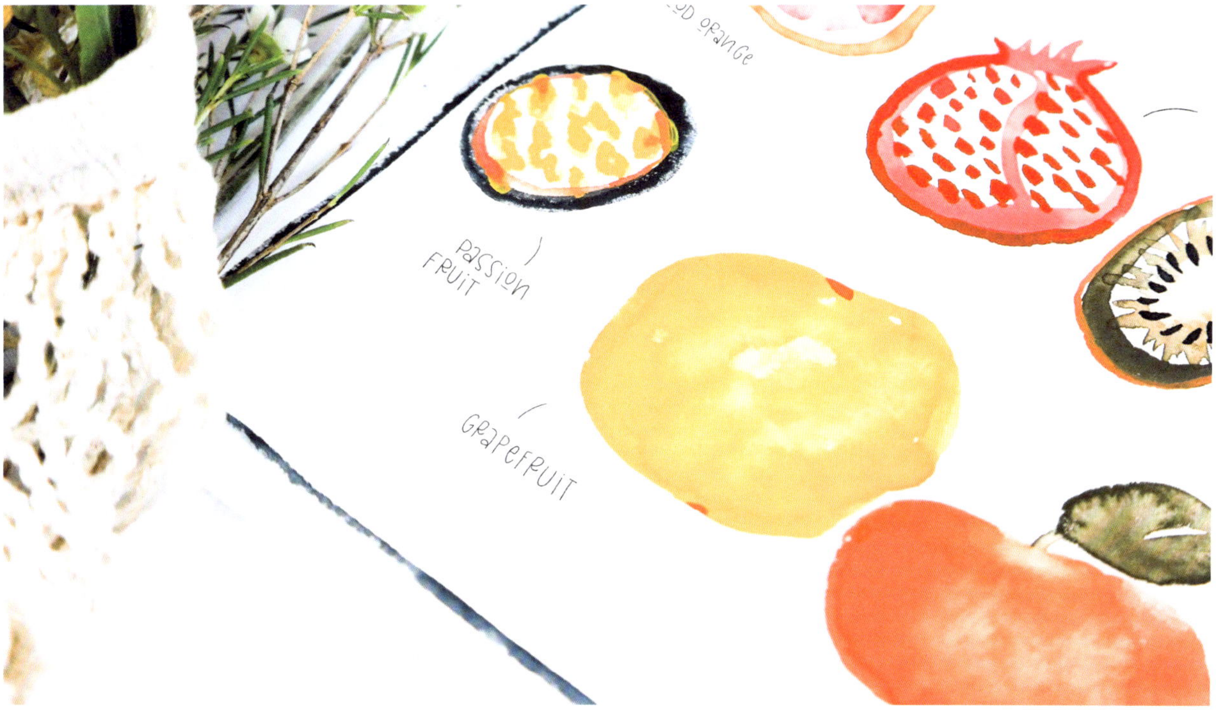

# Recipe cards

In a single creative session, you can prepare a number of blank recipe cards for use as and when you choose. This useful project allows you to use a passion for watercolor and hand lettering in a very practical way. In addition, it will also give you the opportunity to create larger amounts of text in different script styles.

Why not give a set of recipe cards, nicely packaged in a box, to loved ones who like baking and cooking?

## MATERIALS

- Watercolor paper (smaller paper format, e.g. A5)
- Watercolor paint
- Watercolor brush
- Pigment liner
- Brush pen

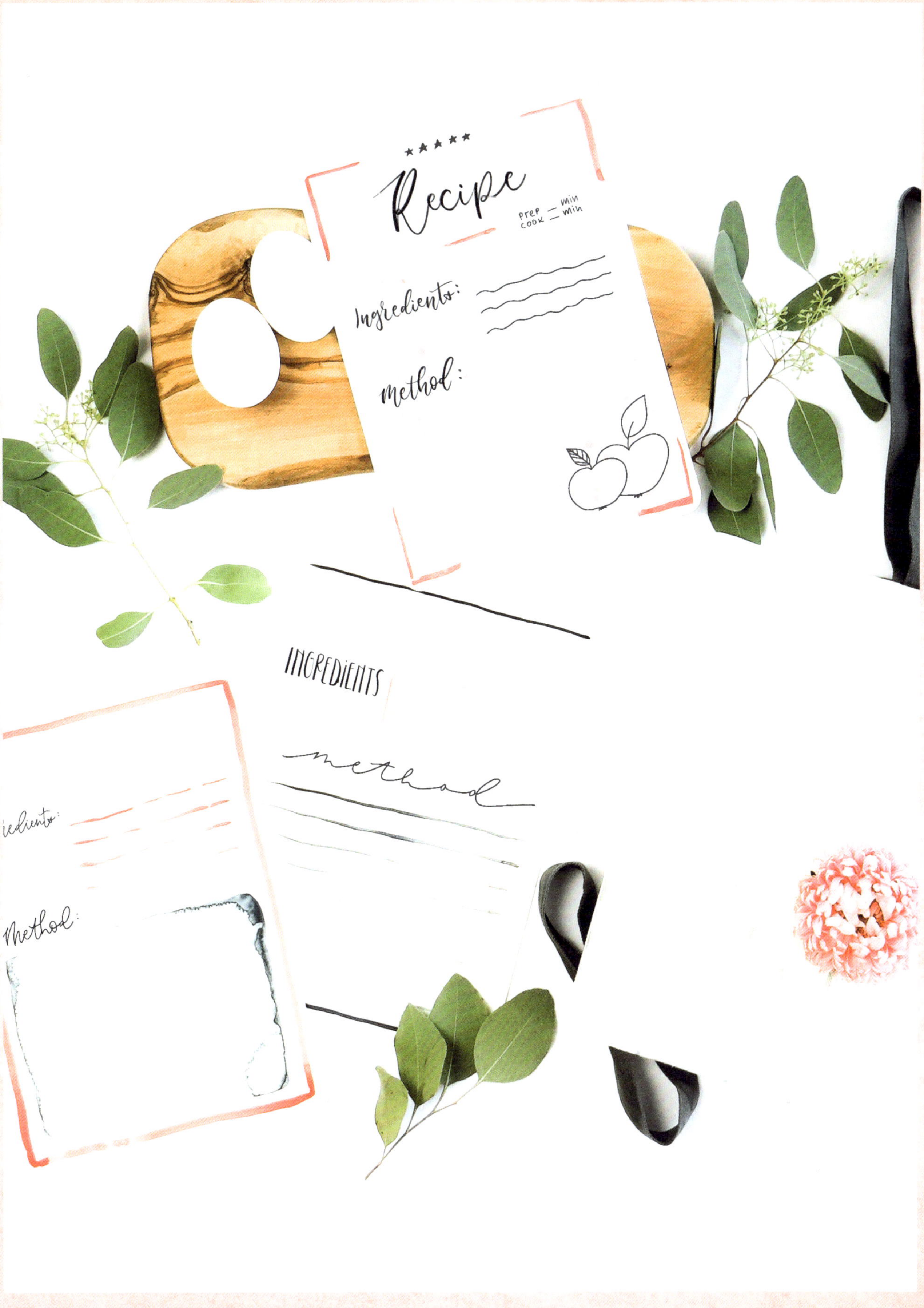
Recipe
prep — min
cook — min
Ingredients:
method:
INGREDIENTS
method
Method:

## Here's how to do it

**1.** Think in advance about what information your recipe cards should contain (ingredients, method, preparation and cooking time, etc.) and whether you want to design the recipe cards single-sided or to use the backs of the cards, too. By planning ahead, you will know how many text boxes you need to create and how you want them to appear. My steps show two alternative styles. Choose two to three colors and start creating the first text boxes (e.g. as lines, as a watercolor area or as a white space area).

**2.** Continue to add the areas as you have planned. You might also want to think about giving your recipe cards frames or other specific boundaries at the edge of the paper, so that they appear more contained (see the finished cards for some ideas).

**3.** When you letter your recipe cards, consider whether you want to use different script styles on each card, or whether all the cards should contain just a few selected script styles, for a simpler and more harmonious look overall.

TIP: *Use the pigment liner to add simple illustrations that match the recipe to be used as decorative fillers.*

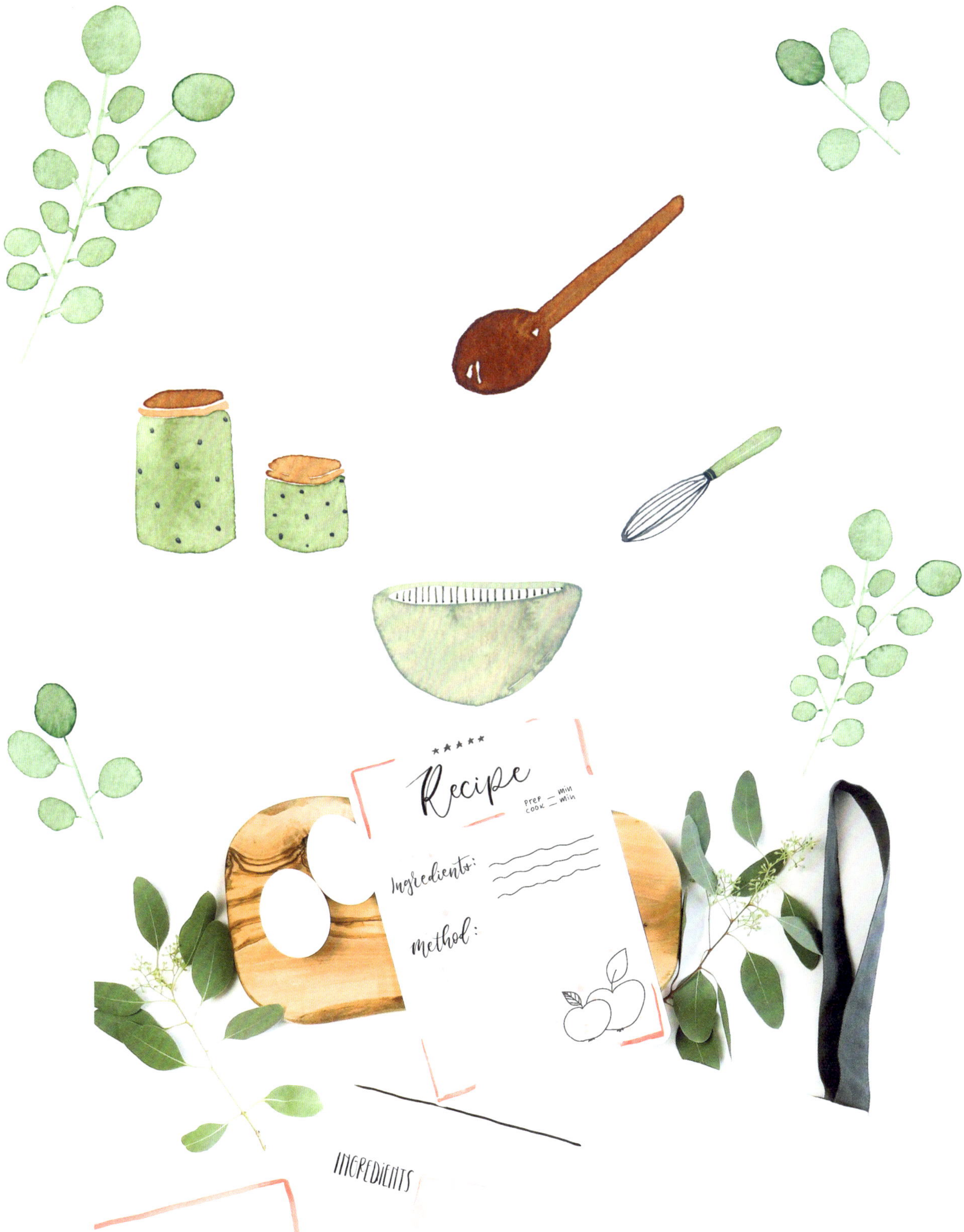
Recipe
prep __ min
cook __ min
Ingredients:
method:
INGREDIENTS

# Birth Poster

This birth poster focuses on the name of the newborn. You can also incorporate other personal details. For example, I chose the zodiac sign as an element in the sky.

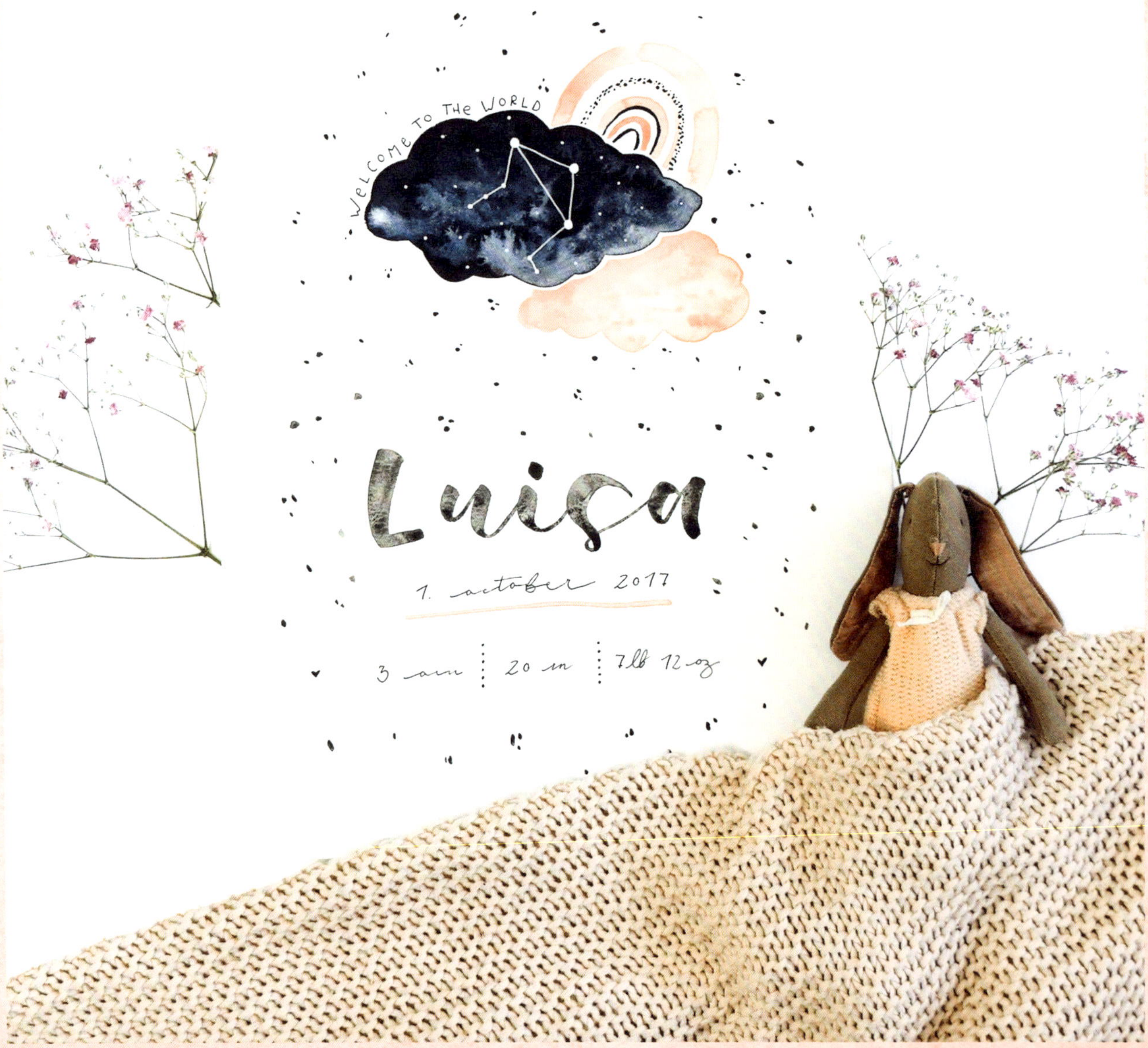

## MATERIALS

- Watercolor paper (larger paper format, e.g. A3)
- Watercolor paint
- Watercolor brush
- Pigment liner
- Gel pen

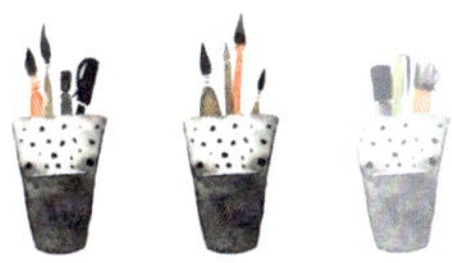

## Here's how to do it

**1.** First decide on what script style you want to use to letter the name, and whether you want to use pens or paints. Experiment on a spare sheet of paper. Remember that the name is the stylistic starting point of your birth poster.

TIP: *I used Schmincke Horadam watercolor paint in Iron Oxide Black (or Mars Black) to letter the name "Luisa". The effects of this watercolor paint are unique in my opinion.*

**2.** Now think about the script style for the other birth information. Consider whether you want to include the zodiac sign, as I have done, or whether you want to use another personal or general topic. Make a note of everything that you want to include.

**3.** Now make little design sketches to work out where to place all the elements. In addition to the name and birth information, choose only a small number of additional items to avoid overloading or even distracting from the name. Also, consciously leave a wider edge to the paper to make the poster more consistent.

**4.** Once you've chosen a sketch, you can now work with your watercolor paints and pens to transfer your ideas onto the birth poster.

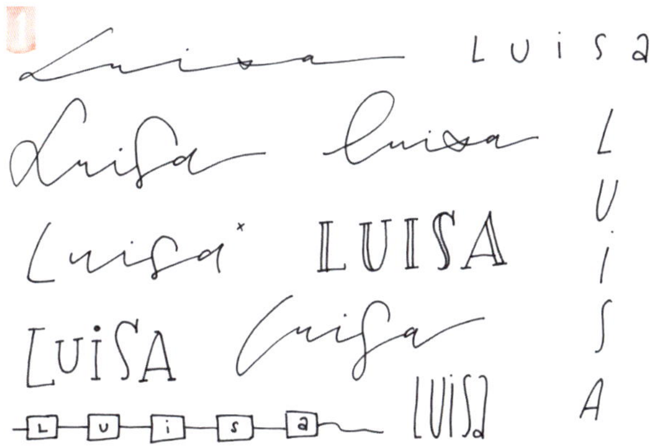


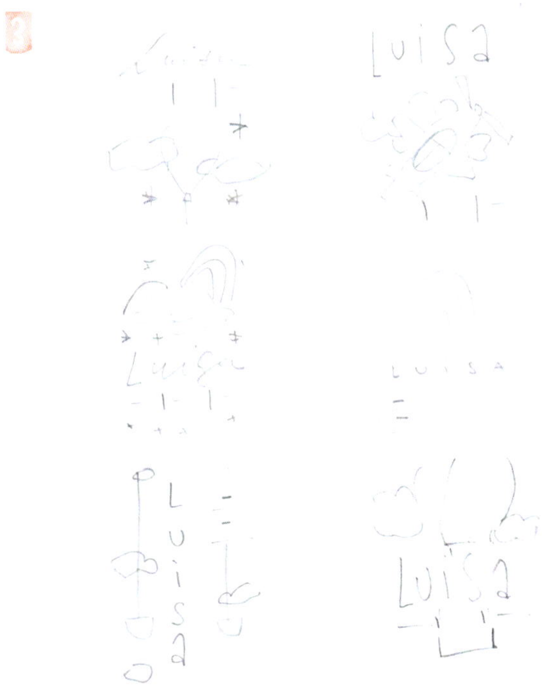

# Milestone cards

These personal milestone cards have space on the back to record all the stages of development in the first few months of life. With this project, you'll be exploring nursery motifs.

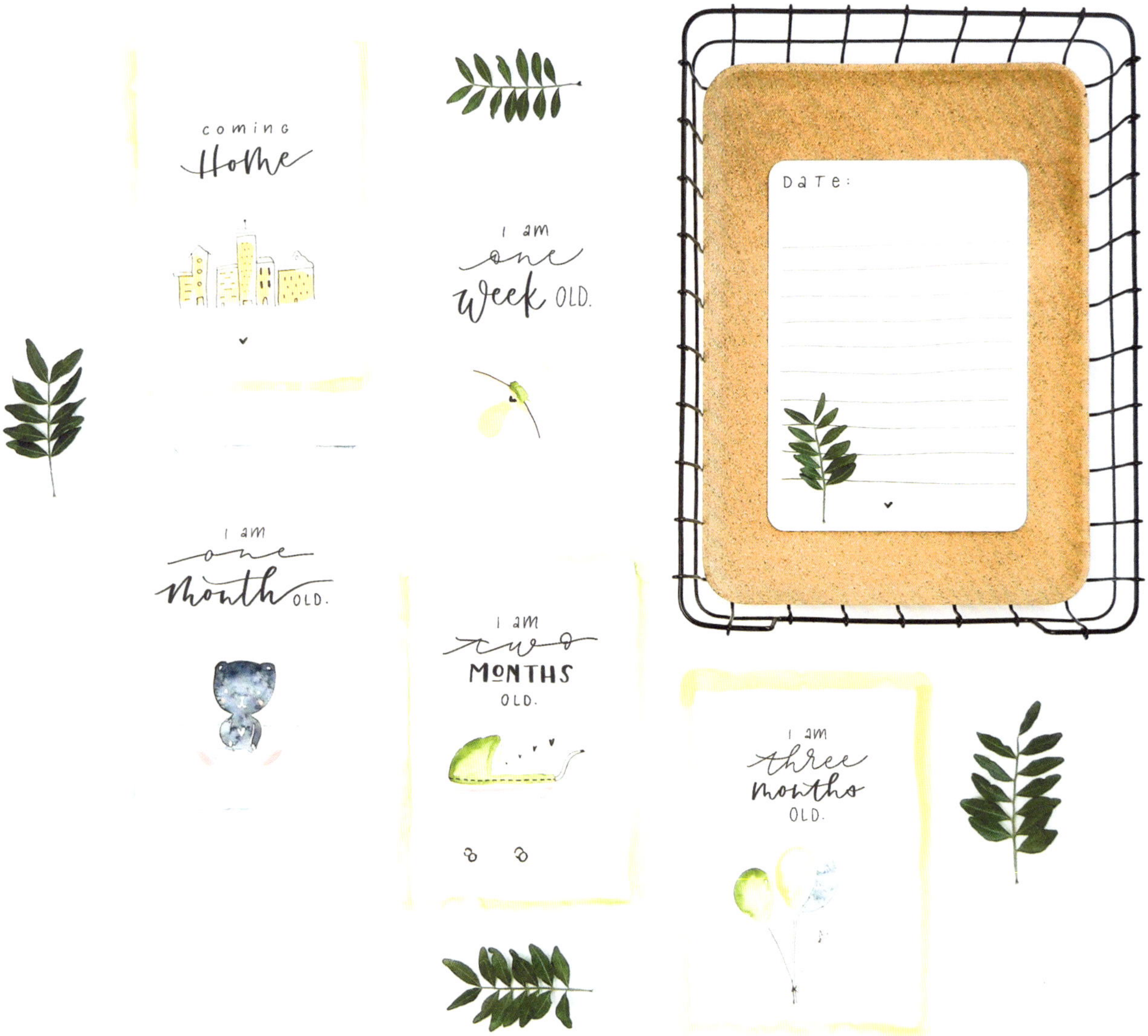

## MATERIALS

- Watercolor paper (smaller paper format, e.g. A5)
- Watercolor paint
- Watercolor brush
- Pigment liner
- Brush pen
- Gel pen
- Corner rounder (optional)

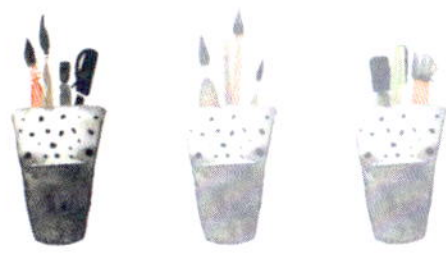

## Here's how to do it

**1.** Decide on the milestones you want to include on your set of cards, and then start lettering them onto each card, leaving plenty of space beneath for your illustration (you can choose one script style for a coherent look or experiment with different ones).

**2.** If the milestone cards are for you personally, you could finish each as the relevant milestone occurs, choosing a motif that seems most appropriate at the time. If, on the other hand, you want to finish all the cards now, I'd suggest two possible approaches. Either you could collect together illustrations of suitable items on a large sheet of paper, a repertoire of milestone motifs for you to choose from, but as far as style, mood, color and representation of these images is concerned, be guided by your creative flow. Or you can jump from card to card, deciding on a relevant object for each milestone and completing a (simple) illustrative design. My step illustration shows how I have painted my individual milestone motifs step-by-step.

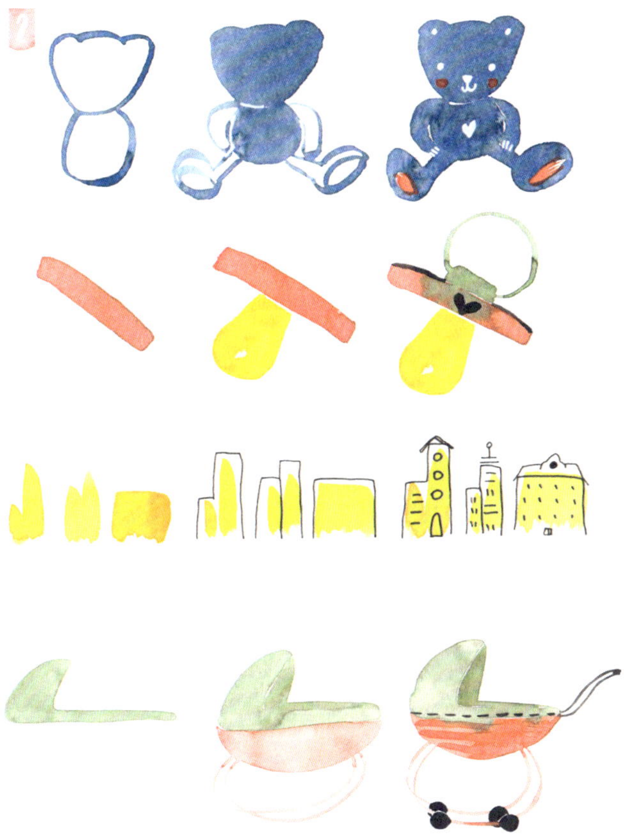

**3.** On the back of the cards, you can mark lines with the pigment liner and make a place to enter the date. For a high-quality finish, you could use a corner rounder if you choose to.

# The big ABC

Children start to get interested in letters relatively early on. Create your personal ABC and you'll be amazed at the enthusiasm it'll spark.

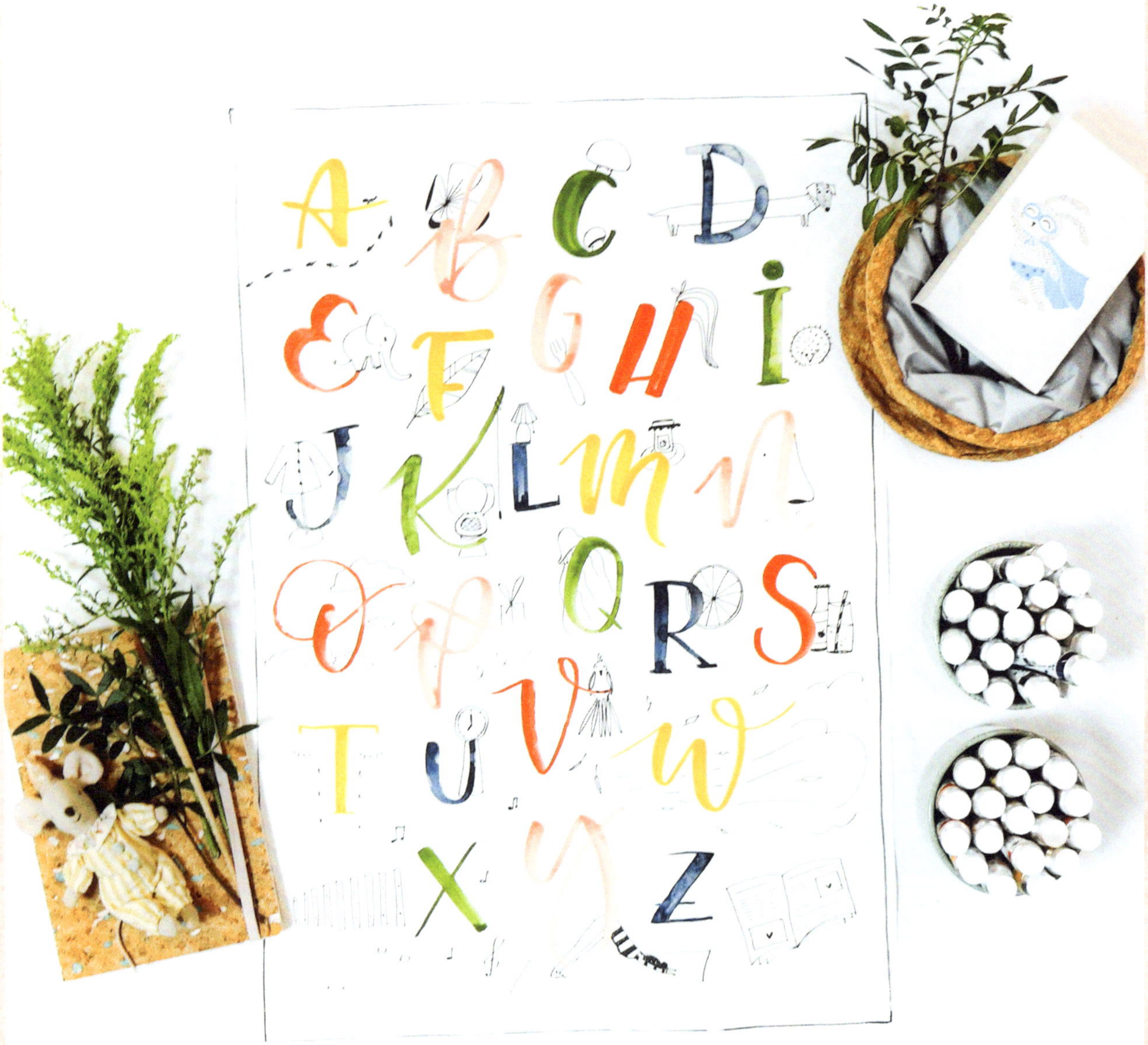

## MATERIALS

- Watercolor paper (larger paper format, e.g. A2)
- Watercolor paint
- Watercolor brush
- Pigment liner

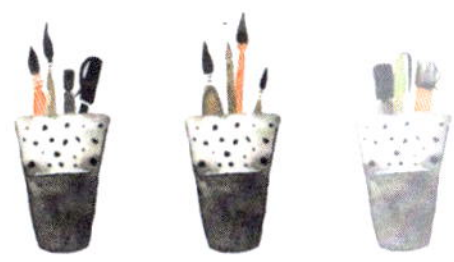

## Here's how to do it

1. Have you put together a color palette and warmed up a bit with the brush? If so, just start lettering intuitively letter by letter – in the style that comes to mind for each particular letter. Don't place all the letters in a row on the line, but position some a little higher, others a little lower. This automatically results in a somewhat more relaxed overall picture. You can choose to add different details and effects to your letters. In my step illustration, I've explored some different ways for rendering the letter "A" .

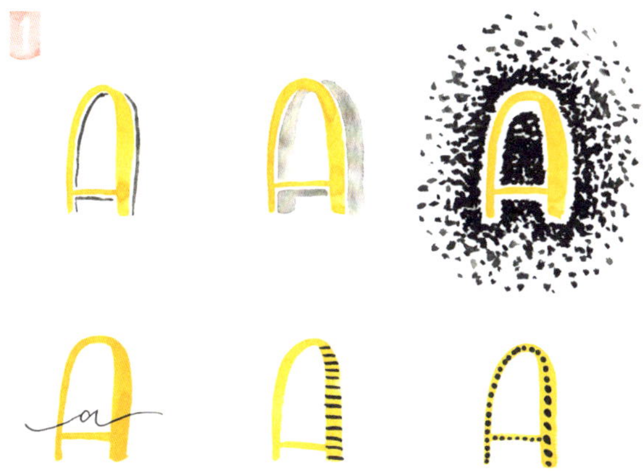

2. Let your letters dry thoroughly and then add an illustration to each using the pigment liner. These could be based on letter associations, such as "A" for ant or "B" for buttercup, or they could be purely decorative, or even a mix of both!

3. Fill any final gaps by expanding individual motifs a bit or by adding details around them (e.g. the bird perching on my letter "V" loses a feather, the wind blowing off my letter "W" swirls the leaves around).

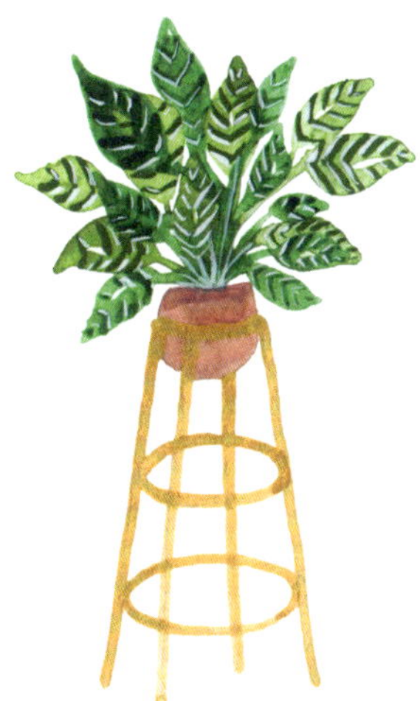

TIP: *Roughly note how the letters should be distributed, so that the entire alphabet has space on the sheet of paper. Then just go ahead and fill in uneven gaps with small illustrations.*

# Picture Wall

Decorate the children's room, or a shared family area, with your own lettered and illustrated picture wall. It shouldn't just be about elegant sayings and popular designs, but also remembering shared experiences and putting those memories down on paper.

This project is all about combining hand lettering with watercolor illustration. Your arrangement will depend on the sayings you select and the images you choose to illustrate your family's stories.

Choose your motifs to best suit the child for whose nursery you may be designing the picture wall.

## MATERIALS

- Picture frames
- Watercolor paper
- Watercolor paint
- Watercolor brush
- Brush pen
- Pigment liner
- Pigment marker (suitable for lettering on glass)

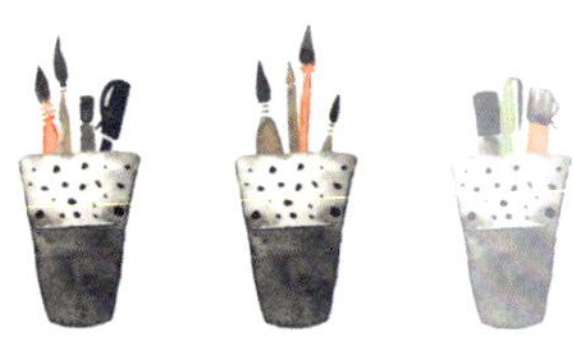

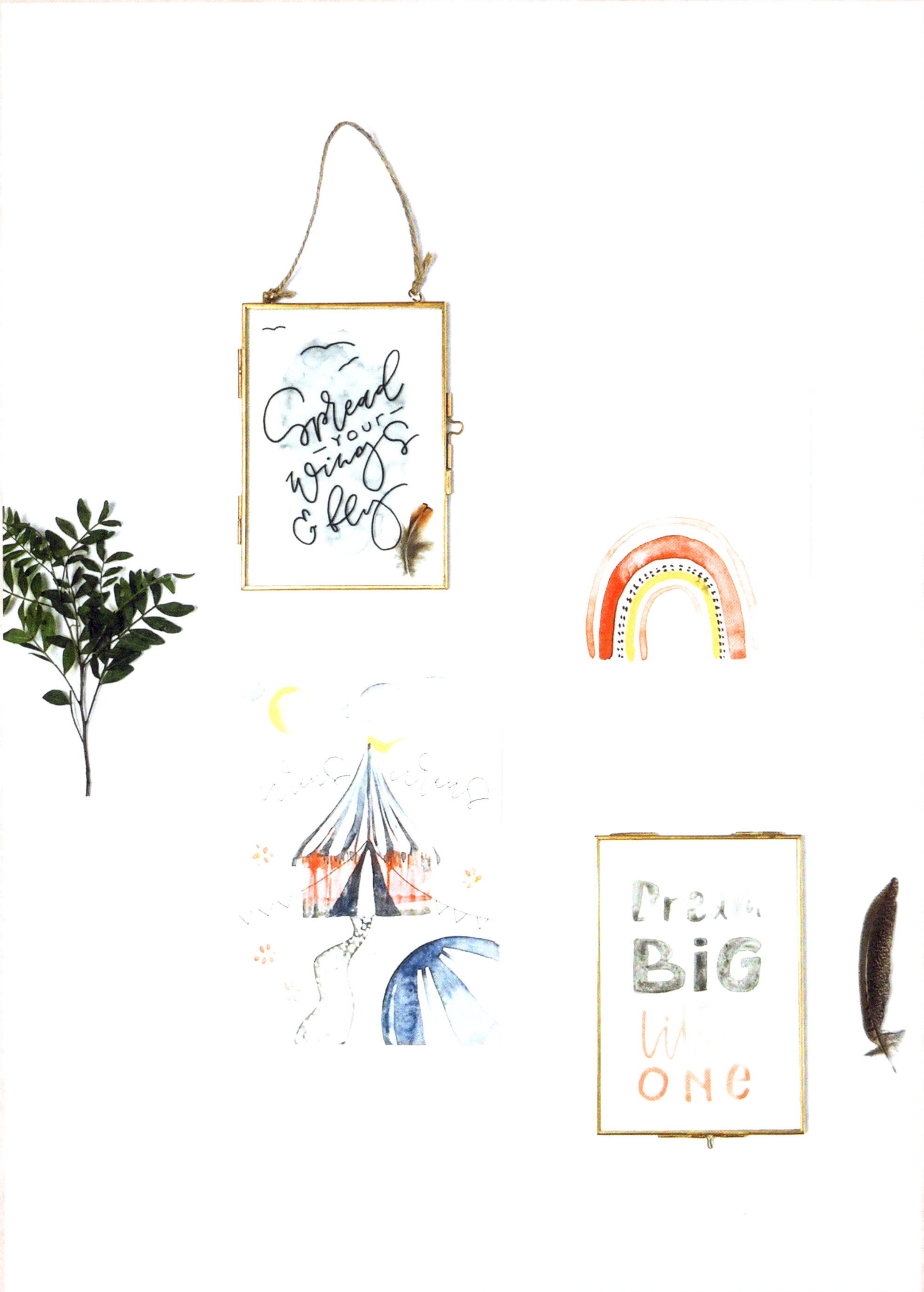
Spread your wings & fly
Dream
BIG
ONE

## Here's how to do it

1. Start by collecting all the picture frames that you plan to use, remembering that you don't just have to frame your illustrations, but that you can illustrate directly onto the picture glass too. Think about what sayings, design ideas and shared experiences you want to use. Then determine which sayings you'll letter, which lettering you'll do on paper or on glass, which you'll decorate with watercolor and which are suitable as stand-alone illustrations for the picture wall (such as the rainbow in my example). Think about what motifs you want to present in a little more detail.

2. Once your decisions have been made, you can start on the individual pieces for your picture wall. When lettering a saying with watercolor brushes and paint, you could indulge in a few deliberate irregularities and inaccuracies for a special childlike charm. For more detailed motifs based on shared experiences, a trip to the circus for example, focus on a maximum of two main objects that you've remembered (in my illustration, I chose a circus tent and a clown's ball). If you want to letter a glass picture frame (as I did using a Uni Posca Paint Marker), you can add an abstract watercolor background within the frame, to match the colors of the other pieces on the picture wall.

TIP: *Not every item needs a picture frame. You can fix some of the pieces directly on the wall with adhesive strips and swap them out as you make new memories.*

3. Once you have prepared all your pieces, hang them on the wall.

TIP: *Try different arrangements for your pictures on the ground before you hang them on your picture wall.*

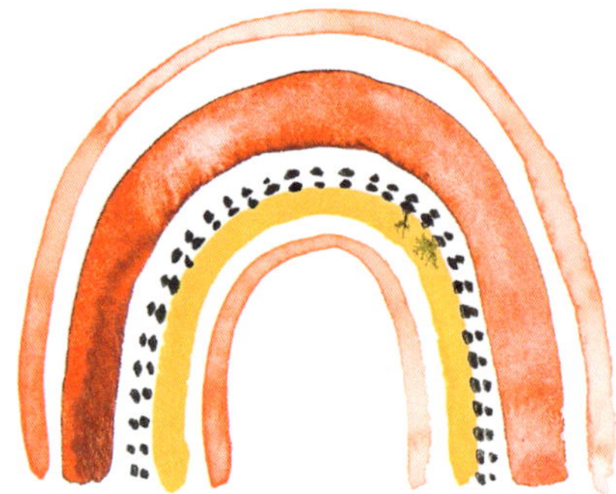

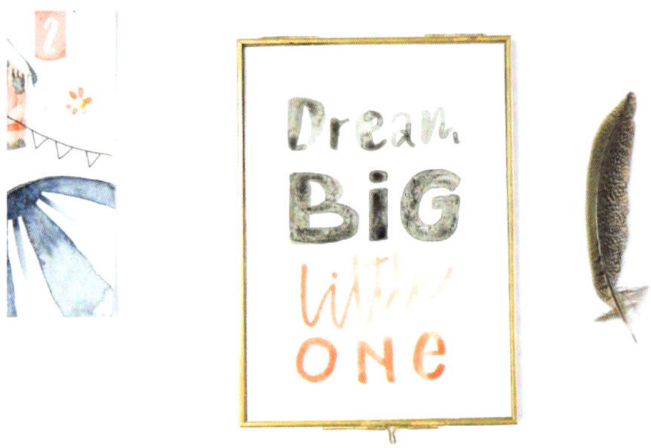


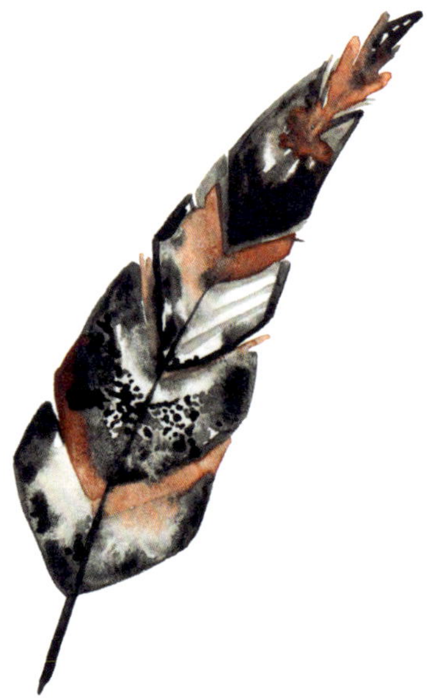

## Inspiration: Adventure and Safari

If you would like to delve deeper into particular motifs, I've prepared illustrations on the topic of adventure and safari as inspiration. You can prepare similar elements for any theme and use them for your picture wall.

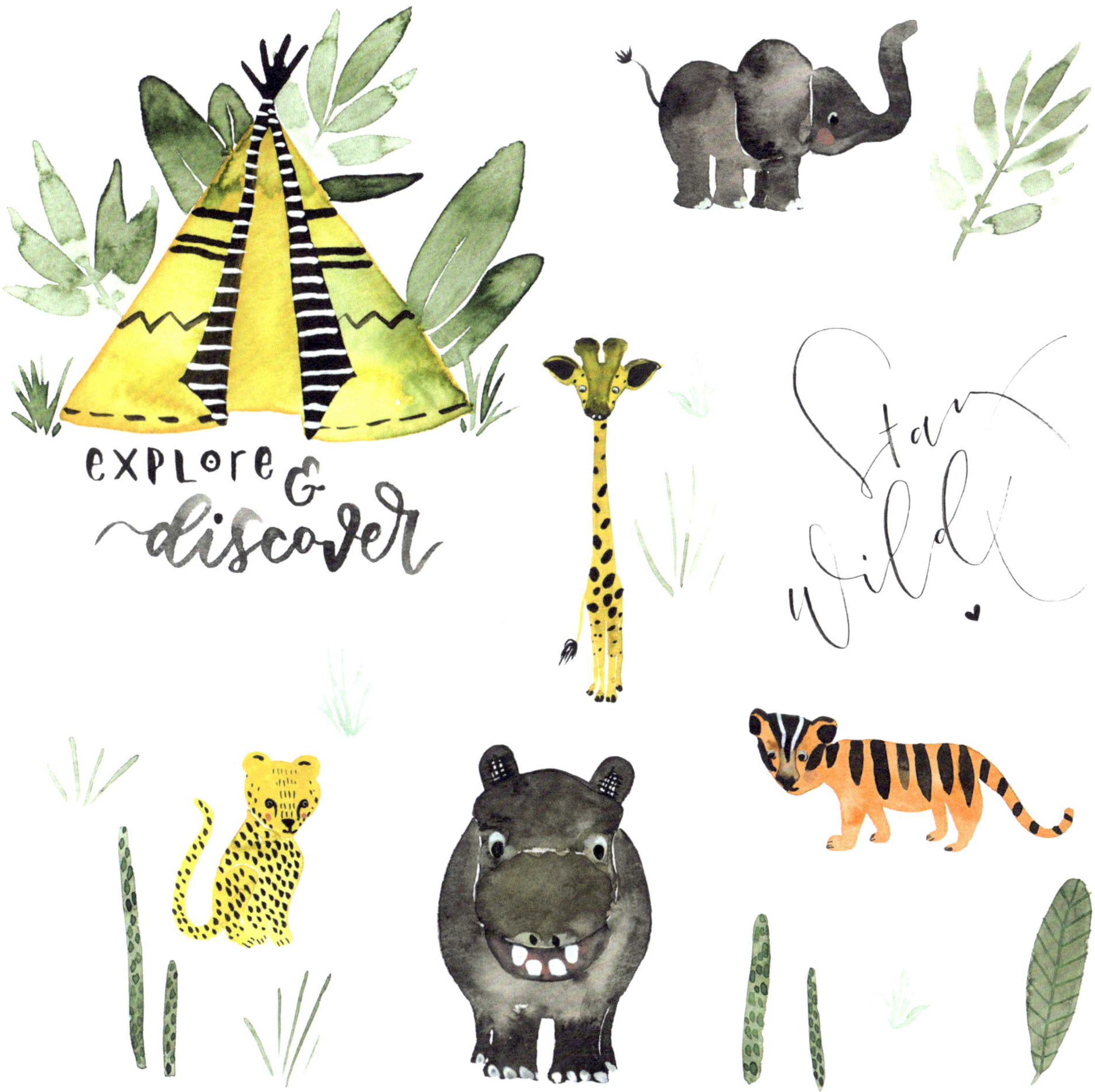

# Height Chart

Create your own height chart for your children from kraft paper and hang it with a matching magnetic picture molding. You'll need to choose a design that can be stretched from bottom to top, and I've decided on a pretty floral motif.

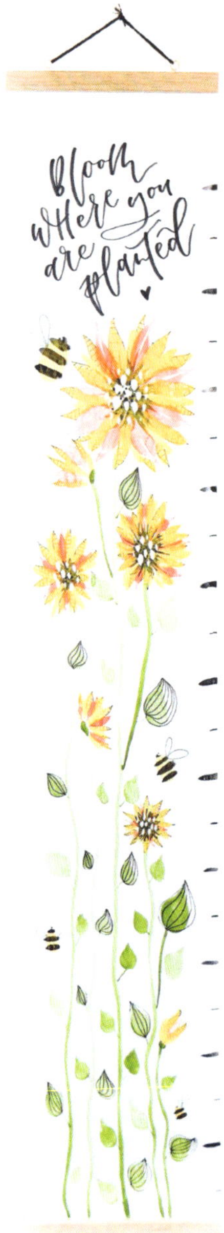

## MATERIALS

- Kraft paper roll (white, approx. 12in/30cm wide)
- Magnetic picture molding (approx. 12in/30cm wide)
- Cord (for hanging)
- Watercolor paint
- Watercolor brush
- Brush pen
- Pigment liner
- Gouache paint (white)

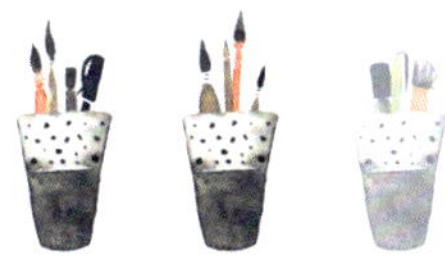

## Here's how to do it

1. Cut a strip from the paper roll to the desired length and clip it into the magnetic picture molding; alternatively, weight the ends of the paper strip, so that it can't curl up during your creative session.

2. Now apply your motif step-by-step onto the paper strip. Always let the paint dry in between so that you don't smudge it. My step illustration shows how I have painted my flower motif step-by-step, including the addition of the bee motif detail. Once I had added all the detailing to the petals and leaves with pigment liner, I painted some large dots in the middle of the flowers with white gouache paint to finish.

3. Now complete the lettering (I've used the Karin Brushmarker Pro brush pen in black for this project), and don't forget to measure and mark growth markers along one edge. Then hang your homemade height chart (at the right height).

2

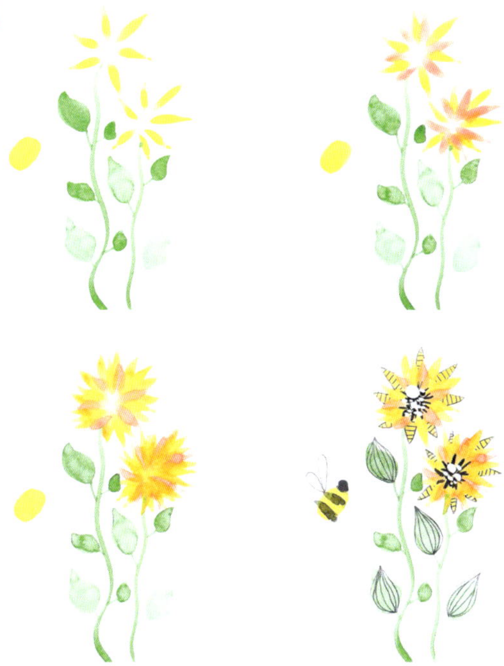

TIP: *Instead of growing flowers, other design options could include a ladder, a rope, a path, a building or even a giraffe.*

# Beetle canvases

This project focuses on gouache paint. The incredible opacity and color density of this medium are unmistakable in my view, and it has a wonderful matte effect once the paint has dried. If you don't have gouache paint to hand, you can easily use watercolor paint if you swap out the black canvas for a watercolor-friendly surface or paper type.

Before you start this project, collect a few photos of beetles and look at their characteristics closely in advance, including body shape, legs and markings.

## MATERIALS

- Gouache paint
- Black stretched canvas
- Mixing palette
- Watercolor brush
- Watercolor paper (for the sketch)

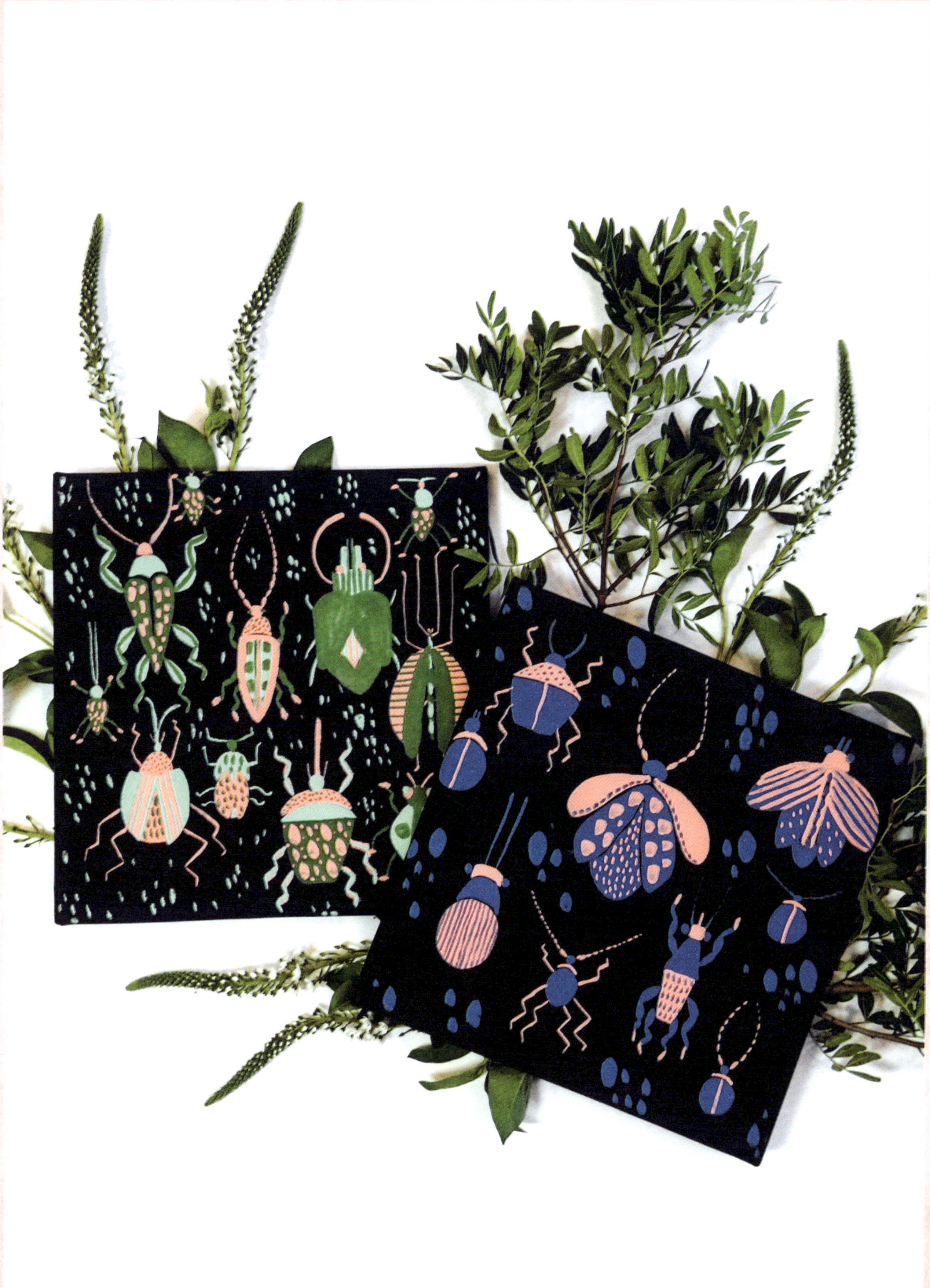

## Here's how to do it

Before you start painting on your stretched canvas, have some watercolor paper to hand – preferably in the same color as the canvas – to test out your color combinations. Put together a color palette – use a maximum of two to three colors at most – and prepare the selected gouache paint in the right consistency by adding a few drops of water to the paint with the brush.

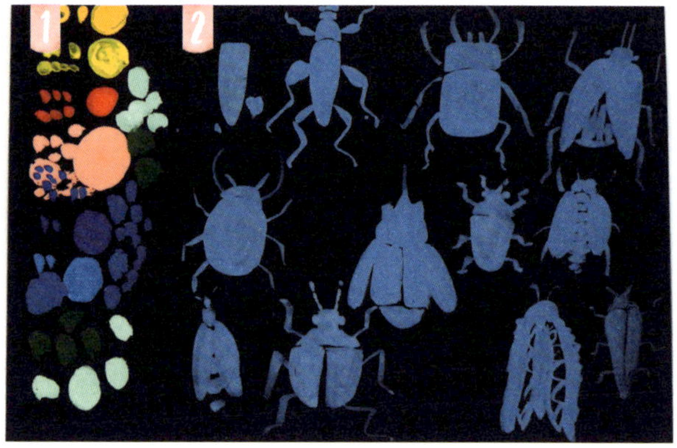


3

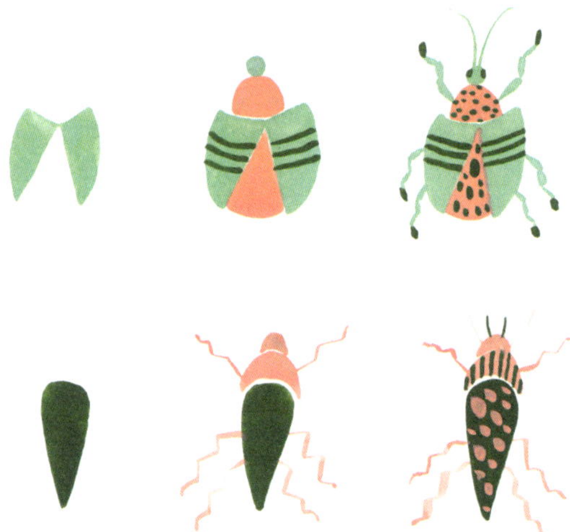

TIP: *Make sure the gouache paint retains its creamy consistency and don't make it too watery. Otherwise, it loses its opacity and becomes more transparent (like watercolor paint).*

1. Use one of your chosen colors to outline a few sketches of various beetle shapes, so that you've a repertoire of motifs to draw from when you begin working on the stretched canvas. Always start with the abstract form of the body, then add details to the body and head and complete the legs and feelers.

2. When you're satisfied with a few of your beetle outlines, start with one color and paint two to three different beetle bodies randomly distributed over the area. Let the paint dry.

TIP: *Leave enough distance between the bodies so that there is space to add the feelers and legs later.*

3. Then take a second color and add a few more bodies (also some with wings). Let the areas dry thoroughly again. Vary the colors and shapes and add head details, then finish with the feelers and the legs, allowing the paint to dry thoroughly between layers. My step illustration shows how I have painted two examples of beetles step-by-step, starting with the body or wings, then adding the pattern detailing as described in step 5.

TIP: *The shape and length of the beetles' feelers and legs are well suited to fill any empty space on your canvas frame.*

4. Once everything has dried thoroughly, you can add abstract markings to the beetles. Fill any remaining empty areas of the canvas by placing an abstract pattern (dots, lines, etc.) between the beetles.

TIP: *When painting markings directly onto the beetles, try to avoid too many brush strokes on the same spot, otherwise you'll dissolve the dried paint underneath – and the colors will easily run into each other if this happens. With just one calculated brush stroke over the already dried gouache area, you'll achieve a clean outline and maximum opacity.*

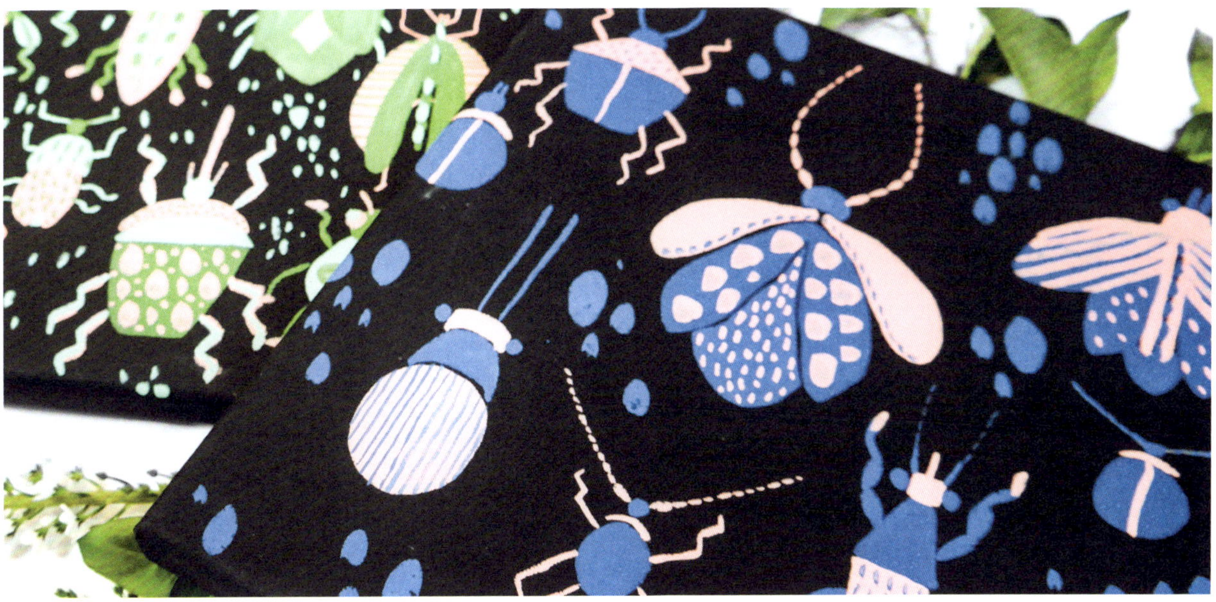

# Moth notebook cover

You can turn a sheet of watercolor paper into a beautifully patterned notebook cover that has the wow factor with just a few snips of your scissors and some simple brush strokes.

Before you start, check that the size of the watercolor paper you have chosen is sufficiently large to cover your notebook as described in step 1.

## MATERIALS

- Gouache paint
- Watercolor paper (max. 120lb/200gsm)
- Watercolor brush
- Mixing palette
- Scissors
- Bone folder or ruler
- Notebook
- Washi (or adhesive) tape (optional)

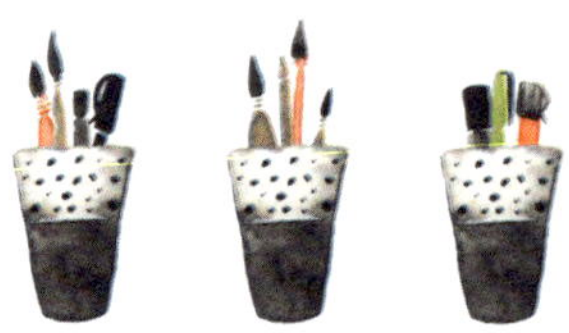

## Here's how to do it

**1.** Check that you have the right watercolor paper size for your notebook. To do this, place your open notebook on the paper sheet and make sure that there is at least 1⅛–2in (3–5cm) of spare paper all around the edge. Next put together a color palette. Then you can start to randomly distribute the moth motifs over the paper, using simple vertical strokes to represent the bodies of the moths. Don't worry about which part of the paper will be on the front of the notebook and which will be on the back. Simply focus on creating the pattern so that it'll end up being harmonious. Let everything dry thoroughly.

**2.** Add various abstract wing shapes. The aim isn't to realistically reproduce moths on paper, but to create them in your own way as intuitively as possible. You'll be amazed by the final result.

TIP: *In order to maintain a more harmonious image from the start, choose a maximum of two to three wing shapes and simply repeat them in different sizes. The more shapes and colors you use, the busier or more crowded the overall picture becomes.*

**3.** Once the wings are dry, you can paint markings on them and on the bodies of the moths. Create these markings with as few brush strokes as possible, otherwise you'll activate the already dried paint surface below and the paints may run into each other.

**4.** Finally, add details such as legs and feelers, then add abstract patterns between the individual moths, so that a holistic pattern is created over the entire sheet of paper without any large gaps.

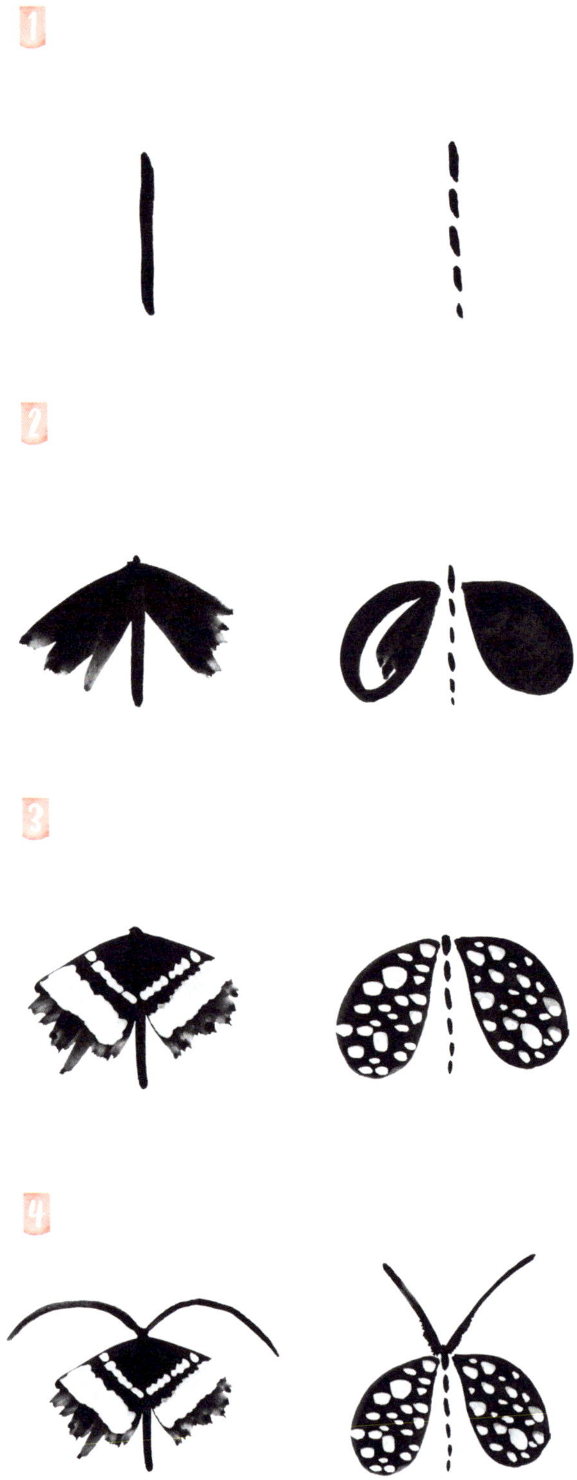

5. Once everything is dry, place the sheet illustrated side down and put the open notebook in the middle of it. To be able to cover the notebook easily, you need to cut a rectangle from each corner of the sheet. Simply use the edges of the notebook as a guide and make the cuts exactly the same height. Make sure that the notebook is placed in exactly the same position each time (reference pencil markings are useful for this). If your notebook is a little thicker, also cut out a narrow rectangle level with the spine of the notebook, so that the paper can easily be folded in step 6.

6. Hold the notebook firmly and fold the paper over to the inside of the notebook cover at the front and at the back. Use a bone folder or ruler to carefully run over the edges of the paper, so that they are smooth. If you choose to, you can attach the folded over paper to the inside of the notebook cover using washi (or adhesive) tape. Close the notebook carefully and rub your bone folder or ruler along the covered spine.

TIP: *You can also use a label to add lettering to the front of your covered notebook.*

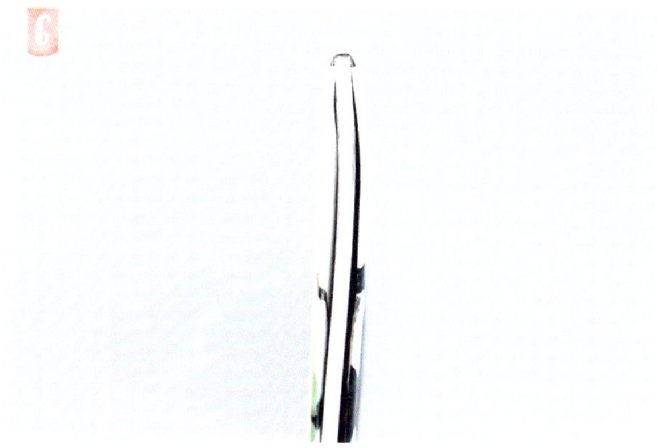


This is what the profile of your covered notebook will look like if you have cut out a narrow rectangular piece of paper level with the spine of the notebook.

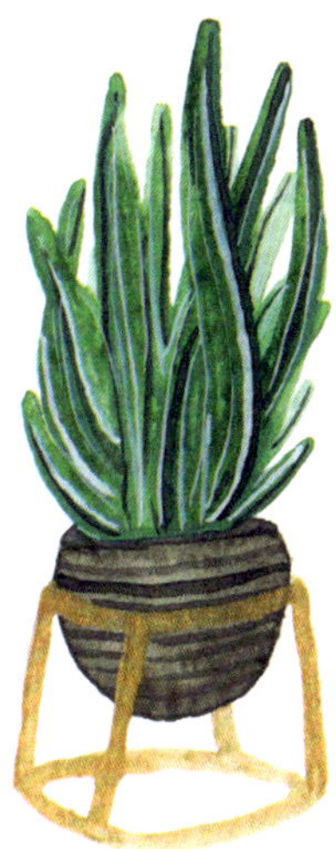

# A bug's life

Here you have the chance to combine the beetle motifs perfected in the Beetle Canvases project with the moth motifs mastered for the Moth Notebook Cover, to create a decorative poster celebrating the insect world. You can take inspiration from other insect species too, but keep them simple.

If you don't have black watercolor paper, you can just use white and work with equivalent contrast by making the lettering and insects black – using color accents that are as transparent as possible when adding any background details, such as the grasses in my picture.

## MATERIALS

- Watercolor brush
- Gouache paint (alternatively: watercolor paint)
- Watercolor paper in black (alternatively: white watercolor paper)
- Mixing palette (alternatively: other smooth base for applying and mixing the gouache paint)

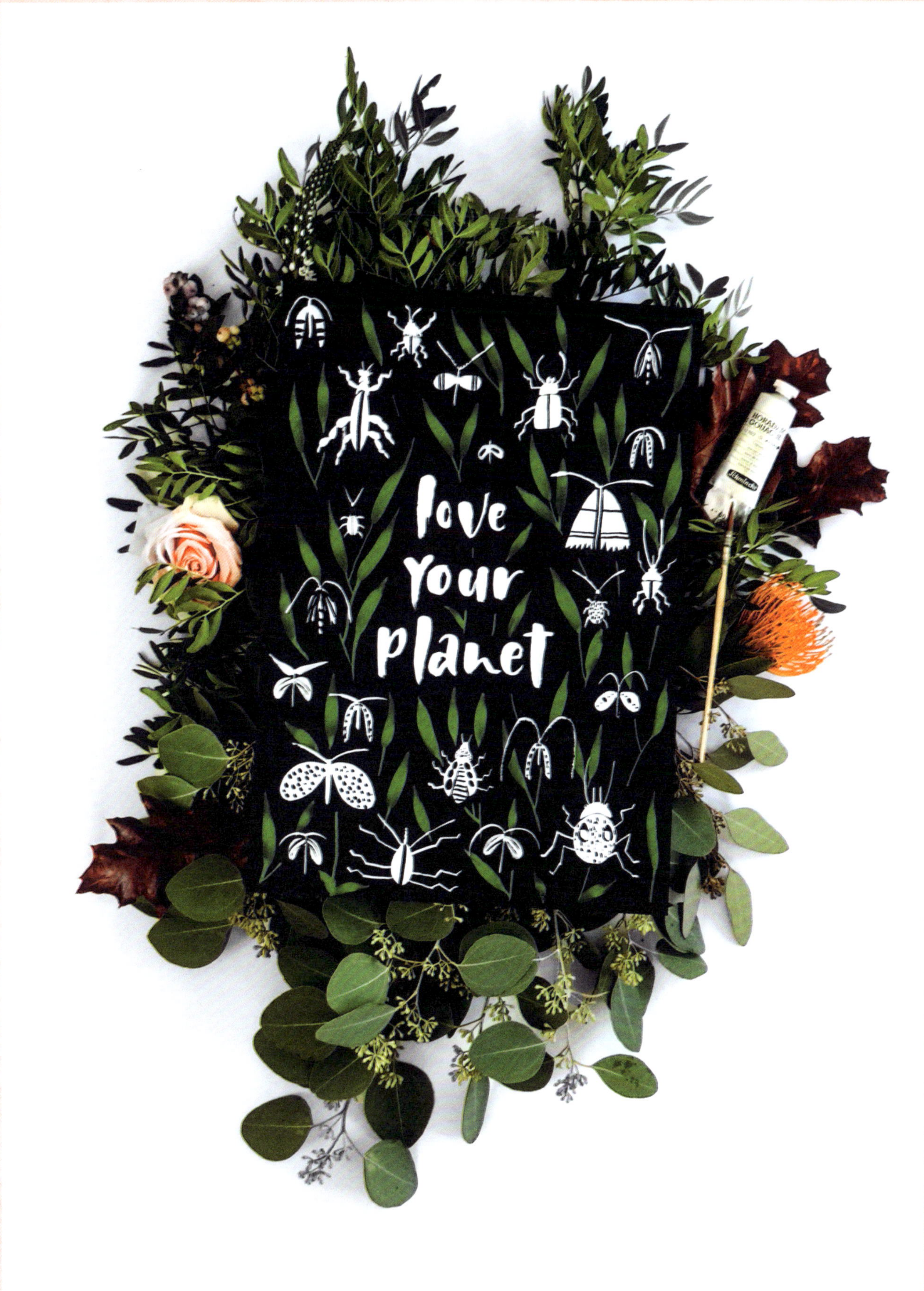
love
your
planet

## Here's how to do it

1. Use gouache paint and a brush to place your selected lettering in the middle of the sheet. Alternatively, you can use a white brush pen or a Uni Posca Paint Marker in white. Leave the lettering to dry.

2. Now you can begin illustrating the beetles and the moths, starting first with the outlines of the bodies.

3. Then add further details, the head, the wings the legs, but don't add the feelers (these will be added at the very end).

4. Now work on the background to fill the gaps in between the lettering and the insects. I have used blades of grass, marking the stems to avoid running through the letters or the insects and placing the leaves in the gaps in between.

5. Once everything has dried, you can draw markings and highlights onto the insect bodies or wings – this time in the color of the watercolor paper, i.e. in black. (If you have used white watercolor paper and created the insect shapes in black, use white for these details.)

6. Finally, add the feelers, painting them over the leaves. Once dry, you can finish the piece by splattering a little gouache paint over the entire sheet, if you choose to.

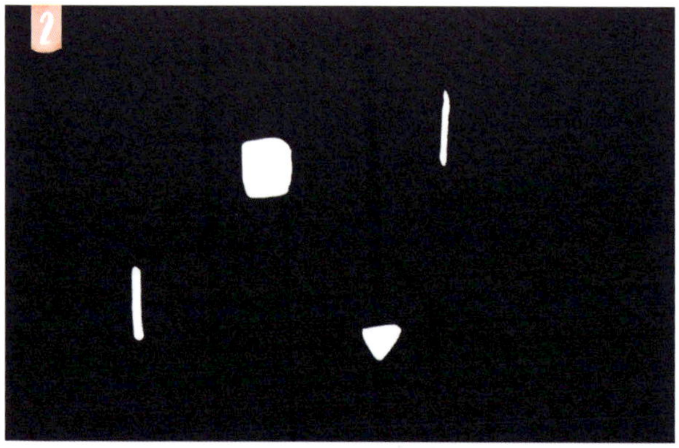


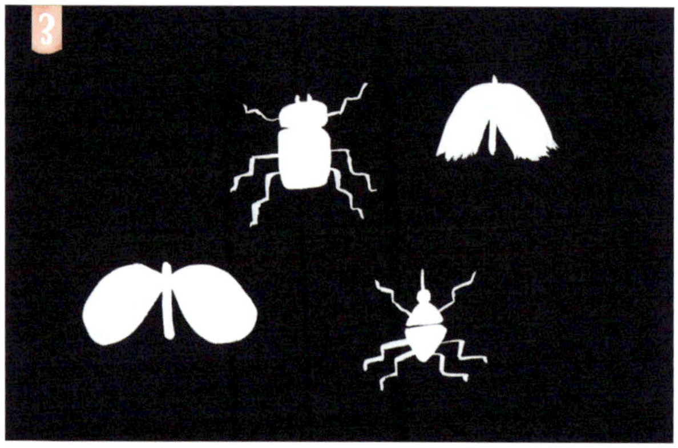


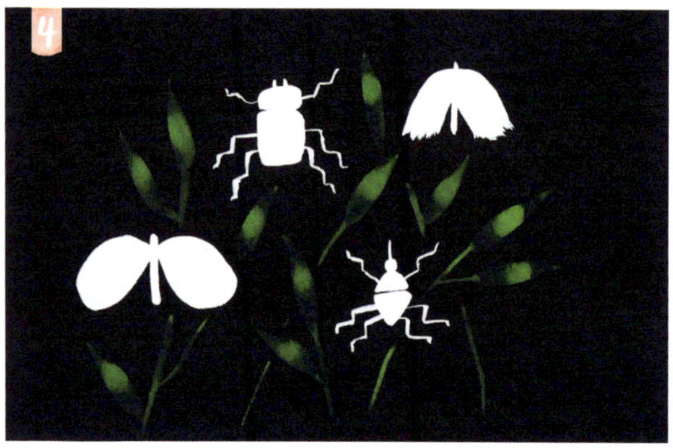

56

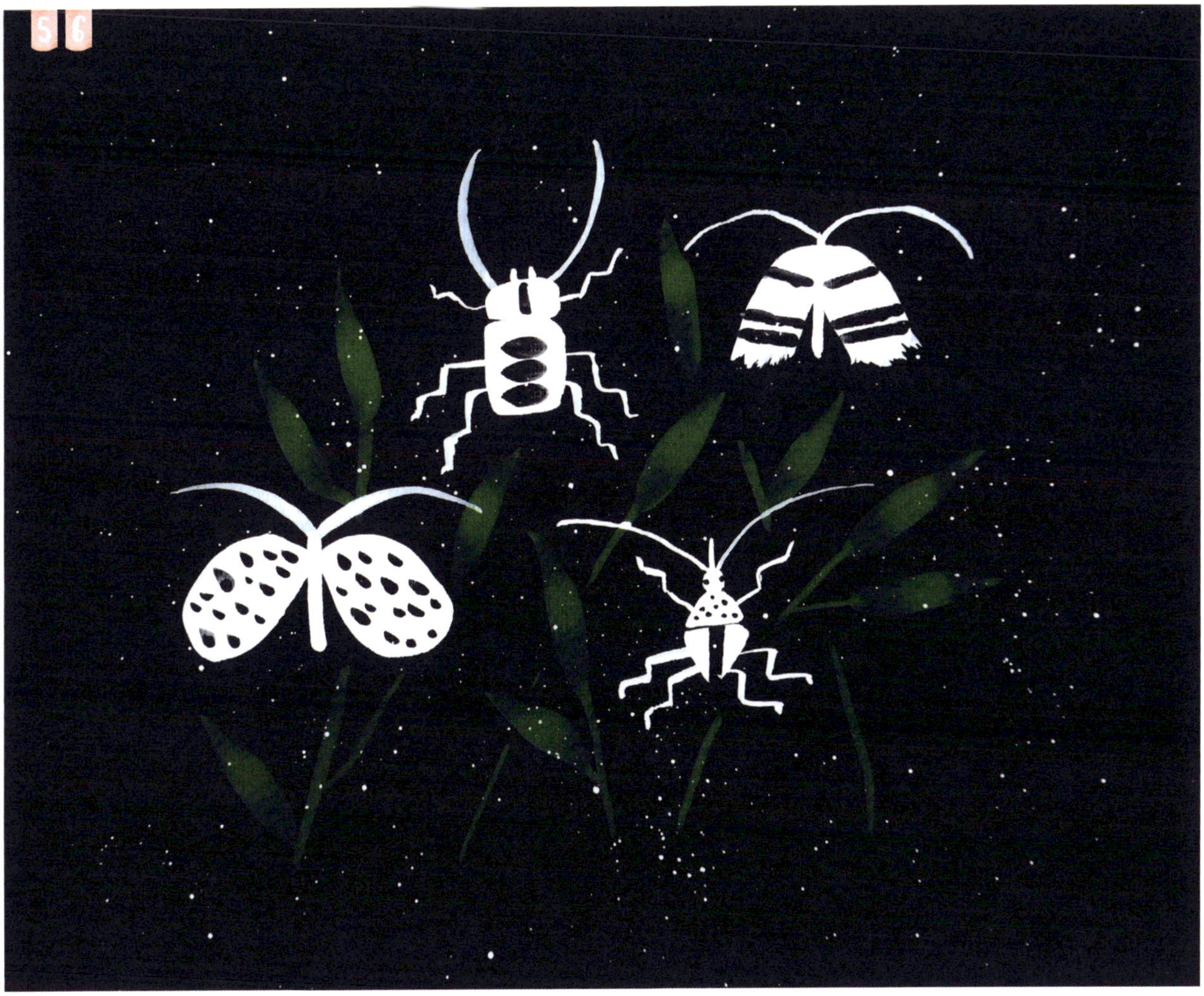

# About the author

Tanja Pöltl is a media and communications consultant and has worked in a media agency since completing her master's degree in 2014. Shortly before her maternity leave in 2017, she discovered hand lettering and watercolor illustration. Self-taught and full of enthusiasm for experimentation, she acquired a lot of expertise as part of a 365-day project, which she now shares in her hand lettering and watercolor workshops. One year after the start of her creative journey, in June 2018, Tanja founded "Die Handletterei". In her creative part-time job, she accepts selected commissioned work and blogger collaborations, while tailoring her workshops to companies and individuals. Building on her expertise on the subject of watercolor, she has also illustrated with gouache since 2019, discovering a passion for digital lettering with Procreate in the same year. Tanja lives with her partner and their daughter in Vienna.

Requests for workshops, commissioned works, collaborations:
tanja@diehandletterei.com

www.instagram.com/diehandletterei

www.diehandletterei.com

Tanja has launched a Lettering Challenge on Instagram:
#letternammorgen

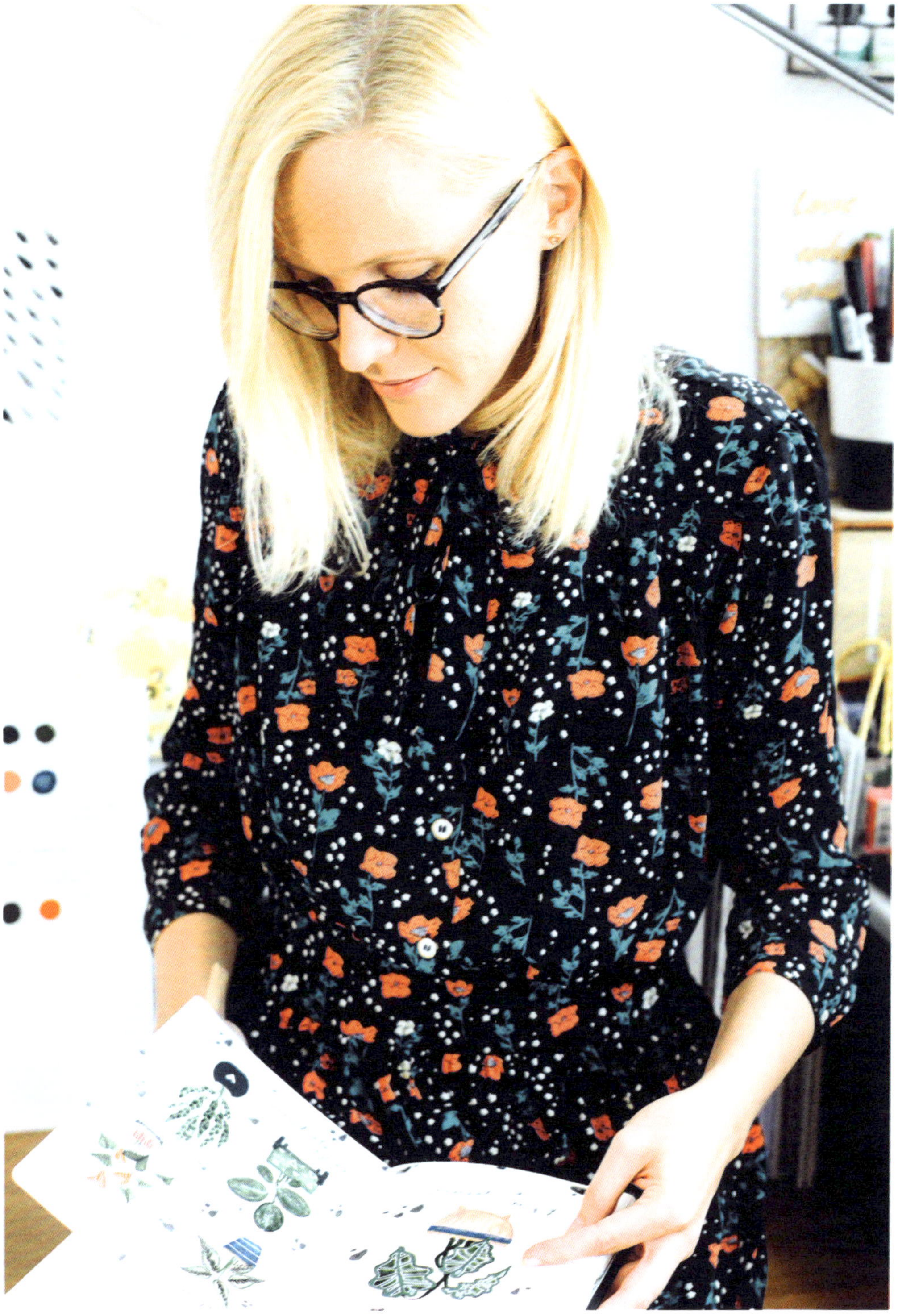

# Acknowledgements

First of all, I should like to thank my life partner, Ronnie, and my parents for their almost indescribable support. Without the time that they've freed up for me in countless ways, this book wouldn't have been possible. Added to this are the words of encouragement, motivation and supportive gestures that have been there from the very start, as well as the support with childcare... THANK YOU from the bottom of my heart!

A big thank you also goes to EMF Verlag, who asked me in the first place whether I would like to work on such a book project. A huge THANKS to my editors, Greta Ruppaner and Anne Hörr, for their fantastic support with this project. Also, for giving me the freedom I needed to write this book right from the outset.

THANKS especially to the Instagram community and all the followers of my Instagram account @diehandletterei. YOU are the reason why I've pursued my hand lettering and watercolor passion up to this point and have now been able to take on such a project. A special thank you (from the bottom of my heart), here, to dear @dianasoriat. You were one of the first Instagram bloggers I followed. Your #30daysdraworletter challenge accompanied me virtually through my entire 365-day project. You could almost say that you are the origin of my creative work - and for that I would like to say THANK YOU.

Last, but not least, I'd also like to thank those people whom I have got to know, not only through Instagram, but also through the monthly lettering meeting in Vienna, who share my passion for hand lettering and watercolor illustration. A very special THANKS to the lovely Nini from @detailors_studio. I've admired you from the outset - not only in terms of your technical knowledge, but particularly for your spirit and your positive vibes :). I not only attended a workshop with you, but actually held one with you. As is well known, people grow with tasks - I definitely learnt a lot from you and with you, and I want to say THANK YOU for that.

# Index

**A DAVID AND CHARLES BOOK**



www.emf-verlag.de

This translation of HANDLETTERING MEETS ILLUSTRATION first published in Germany by Edition Michael Fischer GmbH in 2020 is published by arrangement with Silke Bruenink Agency, Munich, Germany.

David and Charles is an imprint of David and Charles, Ltd
Suite A, Tourism House, Pynes Hill, Exeter, EX2 5WS



First published in the UK and USA in 2021



A catalogue record for this book is available from the British Library.

ISBN-13: 9781446308554 paperback

ISBN-13: 9781446380468 EPUB

This book has been printed on paper from approved suppliers and made from pulp from sustainable sources.

Printed in the UK by Pureprint for:
David and Charles, Ltd
Suite A, Tourism House, Pynes Hill,
Exeter, EX2 5WS

10 9 8 7 6 5 4 3 2 1

Cover design: Silvia Keller, Tanja Pöltl

Editorial and editorial department: Anne Hörr, Greta Ruppaner

Layout and type-setting: Christina Gerg

Translation: Network Languages Ltd

Photo credits:
pages: 18, 52: © r.kathesi/Shutterstock

David and Charles publishes high-quality books on a wide range of subjects. For more information visit www.davidandcharles.com.